Woman Thou Art Loosed

COOKBOOK

VOLUME I

T.D. JAKES

Unless otherwise indicated, all Scripture quotations are taken from the *Holy Bible, New International Version*®. NIV®. Copyright © 1973, 1978, 1984 by International Bible Society. Used by permission of Zondervan Publishing House. All rights reserved.

The recipes contained in this book are to be followed exactly as written. Neither the Publisher nor the Author is responsible for any specific health or allergy needs that may require medical supervision, or for any adverse reactions to the recipes contained in this book.

Executive Director: Rosilyn Houston
Executive Assistant: Sherri Deckard
Production Director: Tom Rutherford
Production Manager: Michael Stiles
Photographs: Russ Harington
Art Director: Chitra Sekhar

Woman Thou Art Loosed Cookbook, Volume I
ISBN 1-57855-998-7
Copyright © 2001 by T.D. Jakes Enterprises, Inc.

Published by T.D. Jakes Enterprises
5787 S. Hampton Road, Suite 445, LB 125
Dallas TX 75232-2200
www.TDJakes.com

Printed in the United States of America. All rights reserved under International Copyright Law. All contents and/or cover may not be reproduced in whole or in part in any form without the express written consent of the Publisher.

ACKNOWLEDGMENTS

Our thanks to those who shared their exceptional recipes to help make this project a success:

Chef Cassondra G. Armstrong	Constance Jenkins
Arthur Bethea	Reginalea "Reggi" Kemp
Cassandra Blakely	Jeumen LeBlanc
Mary Blue	Susan McCarthy
Mickey and Paulette Brooks	Hazel Monplaisin
Ceola Clark	Enetrice Renne Myers
Anitra W. Colston	Jacqueline Nellams
Jon W. Curtis	Elder Johnson Obamehinti
Maye E. Darby	Velma Polk
Ellis Davis	Erica Potter
Phyllis Davison	Annie Merle Price
Gwen DeBrest	Lillie M. Roberts
Saundra Eaves	Toi Lynne Rodgers
Mark E. Finnell	Elders Gail A. & Eddie L. Samuels
Joyce Ford	Linda R. Smith
Chef Carlo Gabrellian	Daisy S. Taylor
Sheron K. Gardenhire	Joan Thomas
Archa Glass	Julie Walker
Lillian A. Hairston-Wheeler	Derrick Williams
Brandi St. Julien Harris	Earnestine Williams
Catherine Henderson	Melvin Williams
Belinda Hopkins	Unetris Williams

A heart felt thanks to all of my friends and to those celebrities who contributed their recipes to make this book possible. Patti LaBelle's recipe reprinted from *La Belle Cuisine* courtesy of Broadway Books, a division of Random House, Inc. Issac Hayes' recipe reprinted from *Issac Hayes Cooking with Heart and Soul* courtesy of G.P. Putnum and Sons.

Special thanks to Chef Anthony Smith, for his unselfish commitment and generous giving of his God-given talents to help unfold the vision for this cookbook.

CONTENTS

Celebrities and Friends	8
Salads, Vegetables, and Side Dishes	60
Seafood	84
Meats and Poultry	96
Breads	112
Desserts	122
International	148

INTRODUCTION

I've been involved in church for most of my life. And if there's one thing I've learned, it's that church people like to eat!

From my Vacation Bible School days (all dressed up in brogan shoes and bow tie), to teen summits and adult conferences, I've discovered almost every imaginable church event calls for some kind of food or refreshment.

Actually, this combination of good food and Christian fellowship isn't new—it's biblical! The Book says the early church continued daily with one accord in the temple, and breaking bread from house to house (Acts 2:46). Many of the miracles in the Bible centered around food. I think we're onto something!

Over the past several years, my wife and I have opened our home to church members, extended family, and numerous friends. We do everything we can to preach a little, laugh a little, and find time to eat, too. Now that our church has grown and God has sent so many special people into our lives, we aren't able to entertain the way we would like to.

But we both still love to do it. So we decided to invite you over for dinner—by gathering some of our favorite recipes and putting them together in a cookbook.

Through the *Woman Thou Art Loosed Cookbook, Volume I*, I hope you will share a meal with First Lady Serita and me. It's our way of saying, "Let's continue, you and I, in fellowship and in the breaking of bread, just the way the Bible says we ought to."

Our prayer is that God will use this cookbook to enable believers from all over the world to break bread together and strengthen the ties of fellowship that bind them. As you use this cookbook, may you be drawn closer and closer to the most important people in your life.

I hope it will be a blessing to you and those you love.

Your servant in the Gospel,

Bishop T.D. Jakes, Sr.

GREEK SALAD

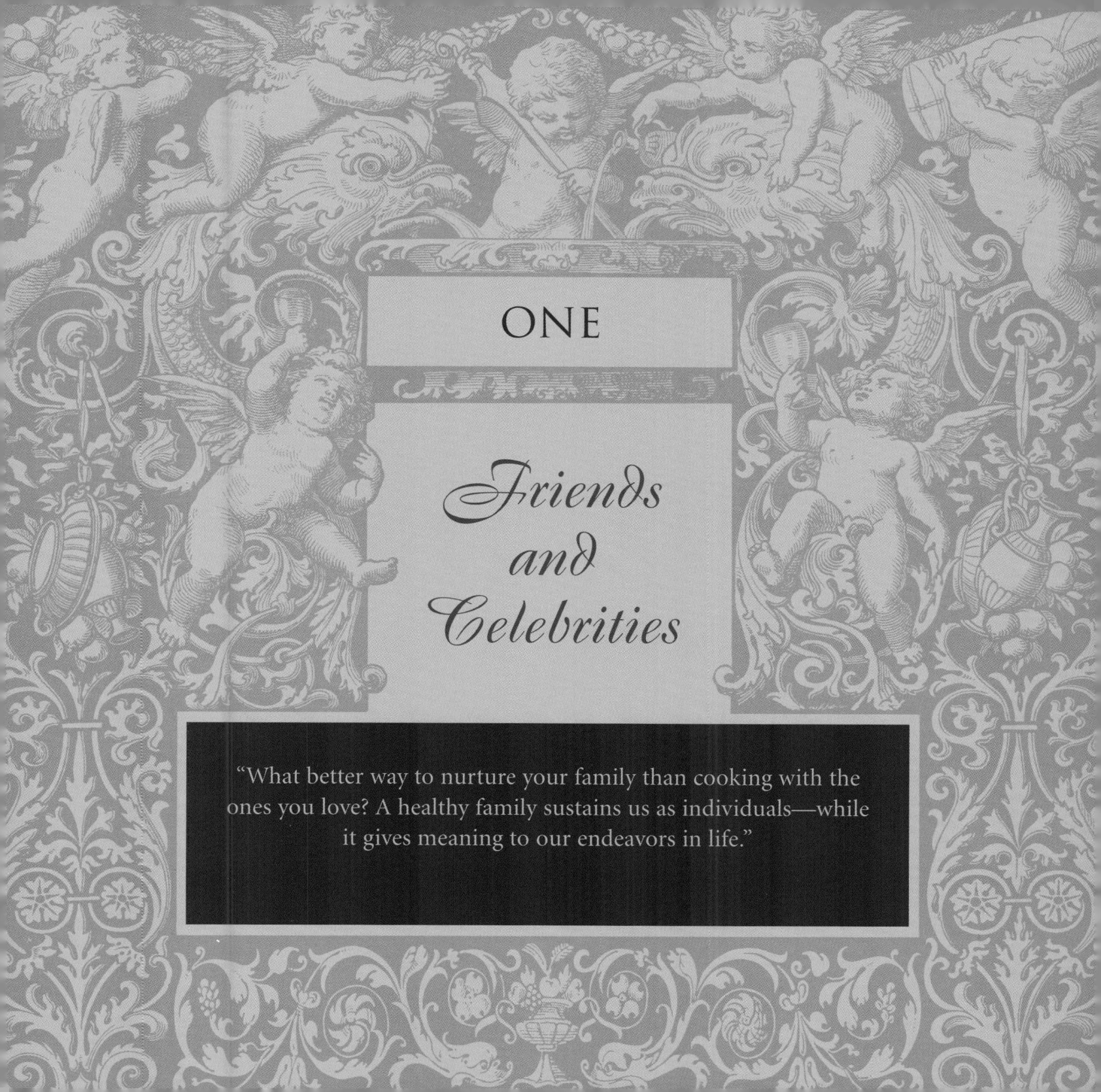

ONE

Friends and Celebrities

"What better way to nurture your family than cooking with the ones you love? A healthy family sustains us as individuals—while it gives meaning to our endeavors in life."

DIVINE SALAD

Contributed by:
Bishop and First Lady Jakes

Number of Servings: 6-8
Preparation Time: 30 minutes

Ingredients

1 pound mixed spring greens
1 cup roasted pecans
1 Bosc pear, sliced
1 (3 oz.) package imported goat cheese
1 1/2 cup Italian bread crumbs
2 cups cherry tomatoes, sliced
2 eggs, slightly beaten
1 cup 2% milk
2 tablespoons extra virgin olive oil
1 bottle raspberry dressing
salt and pepper to taste

DIRECTIONS

In a medium sized bowl add eggs, milk, and pepper, mix well and set aside. Place breadcrumbs in another medium bowl. Take the goat cheese and form into medallions, the size of a quarter. Dip them in the egg wash mixture and coat both sides with the breadcrumbs.

In medium sauté pan, heat the olive oil and cook medallions on each side until golden brown. In a large salad bowl toss spring greens, pecans, cherry tomatoes, pears, and raspberry dressing. When mixed well, top with the prepared goat cheese medallions and serve.

GREEK SALAD

Contributed by:
Bishop and First Lady Jakes

Number of Servings: 6-8
Preparation Time: 20 minutes

Ingredients

1 head romaine lettuce, chopped
1 (3 oz.) can black olives, sliced
1 (6 oz.) jar Spanish olives
1 (8 oz.) jar whole pepperoncini peppers
1 (3 oz.) package herb feta cheese, crumbled
1/2 pound prosciutto (Italian spiced ham), julienne
1 bottle Greek dressing
2 cups cherry tomatoes, sliced

Directions

In a large bowl mix all ingredients together, and toss until dressing has been incorporated thoroughly. Serve immediately.

BROCCOLI CASSEROLE

Contributed by:
Jacqueline Jakes

Number of Servings: 4-6
Preparation Time: 20 minutes

Ingredients

1 (10 oz.) package frozen chopped broccoli
1/2 can condensed cream of mushroom soup
1/2 cup mayonnaise
1 egg, well beaten
l/2 cup sharp cheddar cheese, grated
2 tablespoons chopped onion
pepper to taste
2 tablespoons butter
1/4 cup crushed round rich crackers

DIRECTIONS

Preheat oven to 350°. Cook the broccoli for 5 minutes in boiling water. Drain well. Combine soup, mayonnaise, egg, cheese, pepper, and onion. Mix well. Add broccoli and spoon into lightly greased baking dish. Dot with butter and sprinkle with crushed crackers. Bake for 30 minutes.

MEXICAN CASSEROLE

Contributed by:
*Bishop Terry and
Pastor Renee Hornbuckle*

Number of Servings: 6-8
Preparation Time: 45 minutes

Ingredients

1 pound ground beef
2 cans ranch-style beans
1 large can of chili (without beans)
1 pound package of
Velveeta cheese spread
1 can Rotel diced tomatoes
1 can cream of mushroom soup
1 bag Tostitos bite size chips

Directions

Preheat oven to 350°. Brown ground beef. Drain away access fat.

Layer bottom of a casserole dish with tortilla chips. Make sure the bottom is completely covered. Spread cooked ground beef on top of the chips and layer ingredients in the following order: ranch beans, chili, and cheese.

In a bowl, mix Rotel tomatoes and cream of mushroom soup. Spread this mixture on top.

Cook for 45 minutes.

FRIENDS AND CELEBRITIES

VICKIE'S "TOP SECRET" DRESSING

Contributed by:
Vickie Winans

Number of Servings: 6-8
Preparation Time: 1 hour

Ingredients

1 to 1 1/2 teaspoons sage, or to taste
3/4 cup chopped green pepper
3/4 cup chopped onion
1/2 cup chopped celery
2 boxes Jiffy cornbread mix
3 to 3 1/2 pounds Italian hot sausage, rope style
gizzards and neck, from chicken or turkey

Directions

In a small saucepan, cook the gizzards and neck in water. Save broth. Cut meat from bones and set aside.

Place whole sausage in a large fry pan and smother with chopped vegetables. Cook over medium heat until sausage is almost done. If desired, pour 1/2 cup water over sausage to start cooking. Save all juices.

While sausage is cooking, prepare Jiffy cornbread mix according to directions. Bake until golden; cool.

Cut cooked sausage into small pieces. Place in large bowl. Crumble cooled cornbread over sausage. Add sage and cooked vegetables. Add gizzard and neck meat. Pour broth and juices over the mixture, just enough to moisten. Mix well and put in a large casserole dish. Cook in the oven under the broiler for 5 minutes to brown and crisp top. Serve.

COCONUT RICE

Contributed by:
Pastor Ghandi

Number of Servings: 4
Preparation Time: 1 hour, 30 minutes

Ingredients

2 pints coconut milk
2 pounds rice
10 ounces fresh shrimp
4 magi cubes
4 ounces fresh tomatoes
2 ounces of meat
salt to taste
6 small peppers
4 ounces onion

Directions

Boil the coconut milk for about 10 minutes. Add the cooked meat, cleaned shrimp, and magi cubes. Chop the tomatoes, onions, and pepper and add to the meat mixture. Parboil the rice and add to the boiling coconut milk.

Cook the rice until soft, about 40 minutes. Reduce heat and simmer until the liquid is absorbed. Garnish with carrots and green pepper or peas, and serve.

GROUNDNUT SOUP

Contributed by:
Pastor Ghandi

Number of Servings: 6
Preparation Time: 1 hour, 30 minutes

Ingredients

4 ounces roasted ground nut paste
2 pounds meat
8 ounces fresh fish
1/2 ounce of pepper
8 ounces tomatoes
1/2 okro (optional)
1 1/2 pints water
10 tablespoons palm oil
1 tablet of magi super
4 ounces onion
salt to taste

Directions

Wash, season, and boil meat for 40 minutes, until soft. Chop onion, tomatoes, and pepper. Heat the oil in a large pot, and add the chopped vegetables. Cover the pot and cook for about 15 minutes.

Add the cooked meat, fish, and magi super and cook for 5 minutes. Stir in the groundnut paste. Cook for another 15 minutes. Stir and add salt to taste. Serve with eko (cold steamed pap), or boiled white rice.

QUICK AND EASY FRUIT SALAD

Contributed by:
Pastor Ron Smith

Number of Servings: 6-8
Preparation Time: 20 minutes

Ingredients

1 medium can fruit cocktail
1 medium can pineapple bits
2 small cans mandarin oranges
1 (8 oz.) container sour cream
1 (8 oz.) container strawberry and banana yogurt
2 cups miniature marshmallows

DIRECTIONS

Drain some juice from each can of fruit used and place all of the fruit in a large bowl.

In a separate bowl, blend the sour cream and yogurt together. Fold into the fruit mixture. Sprinkle the miniature marshmallows over mixture, 1 cup at a time. Once all the marshmallows have been added, take a large spoon and spread evenly over the fruit and yogurt mixture.

Chill salad in the refrigerator, from 1 to 2 hours to overnight, and serve.

SCREAMIN' MEAN GREENS

Contributed by:
Patti LaBelle

Number of Servings: 4-6
Preparation Time: 1 hour

Ingredients

5 pounds assorted greens (collard, kale, mustard, and turnip greens, in any combination), tough stems discarded
2 medium onions, chopped
1/4 cup vegetable oil
2 jalapenos, seeded and minced, optional
1 (1 1/2 pound) smoked turkey wing
seasoning salt
freshly ground black pepper

Directions

Tear the greens into large pieces. Wash the greens well in a sink full of cold water. Lift the greens out of the sink and transfer to a large bowl, leaving the grit to fall to the bottom of the sink. (Be sure you get all the grit out of the greens. If necessary, wash again.) Do not drain the greens in a colander.

In a large pot, combine the onions, 2 cups water, oil, and jalapenos, if using. Bring to a boil over high heat. Gradually stir in the greens, allowing each batch to wilt before adding more greens. Bury the turkey wing in the greens. Season with salt and pepper to taste.

Cover and reduce the heat to medium-low. Cook, stirring occasionally, just until the greens are tender, about 30 minutes. Do not overcook the greens or they will lose their color and fresh flavor. Remove the turkey wing. Discard the skin and bones, chop the turkey meat, and return to the pot. Using a slotted spoon, transfer the greens to a serving dish. Serve hot.

SWEET AND CHEESY MACARONI AND CHEESE

Contributed by:
Mrs. Walter Thomas

Number of Servings: 8
Preparation Time: 20 minutes

Ingredients

1 (12 oz.) package Mueller's Ready Cut Macaroni
1 1/2 pounds Velveeta cheese
10 ounces evaporated milk
10 ounces warm water
4 tablespoons margarine
5 tablespoons sugar
1/2 teaspoon pepper

Directions

Preheat oven to 350°. Cook macaroni according to package directions.

Cut cheese and margarine into cubes and place in the bottom of an 8-inch square baking dish. When macaroni is ready, drain water and reserve 10 ounces. Spoon the macaroni into dish on top of cheese and margarine. Add milk, reserved water, pepper, and sugar, and mix well.

Cook until golden brown.

FRIENDS AND CELEBRITIES

SOUTHERN CHILI

Contributed by:
Subrenia McDaniel

Number of Servings: 4-6
Preparation Time: 45 minutes

Ingredients

1 small onion
1 small can of pork and beans
1 pound ground beef
3 tablespoons sugar
1 teaspoon chili powder
2 cups ketchup
2 tablespoons hot sauce
1 tablespoon seasoning salt

Directions

In a medium frying pan, brown ground beef and onion. Drain excess fat and remove from frying pan. Transfer browned ground beef and onions to medium saucepan and add all remaining ingredients.

Cook for 15-20 minutes over low heat. Stir occasionally to prevent sticking. Serve hot.

Best served on hot dogs or over rice.

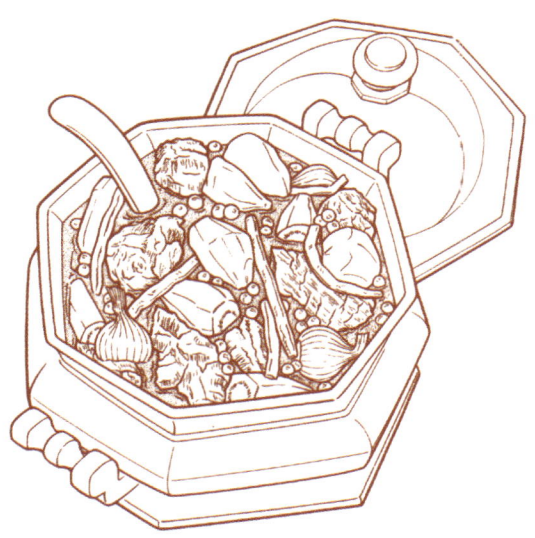

CHICKEN SOUP VENEZIA

Contributed by:
Bishop and First Lady Jakes

Number of Servings: 4
Preparation Time: 50 minutes

Ingredients

1 chicken breast, boneless and skinless
salt and pepper to taste
1 teaspoon garlic powder
fat-free, nonstick cooking spray
2 stalks broccoli, cut in pieces
4 small onions, diced
1 cup baby carrots, cut in pieces
6 cups water
2 teaspoons fat-free chicken broth
fresh parsley

Directions

Roast chicken with salt, pepper, and garlic. Cut chicken into cubes. Spray a large saucepan with nonfat, nonstick spray and sauté vegetables over medium heat. Add water, broth, and chicken, mixing well. Add salt and pepper to taste. Boil 15 minutes on low heat. Serve soup topped with a sprig of parsley.

FRIENDS AND CELEBRITIES

Stuffed Cannelloni with Spinach

Contributed by:
Bishop and First Lady Jakes

Number of Servings: 4
Preparation Time: 30 minutes

Ingredients

1 cup spaghetti sauce
8 slices fat-free bacon
fat-free, nonstick cooking spray
1 teaspoon minced garlic
2 bags fresh spinach
1 teaspoon Italian herbs
1 bag cannelloni
2 teaspoons fat-free Parmesan cheese

Directions

Cook bacon according to package directions. Drain excess fat, crumble into small pieces, and set aside.

Using fat-free, nonstick cooking spray, sauté the garlic, spinach, and herbs in a medium saucepan. Once spinach is cooked, mix in the crumbled bacon. Fill each cannelloni with the spinach mixture.

Heat the spaghetti sauce and spoon over the stuffed cannelloni. Serve topped with Parmesan cheese.

FAVORITE SEAFOOD QUICHE

Contributed by:
Bishop Earnestine Reems

Number of Servings: 6-8
Preparation Time: 1 hour

Ingredients

2 pounds crabmeat
1 pound baby shrimp
2 bell peppers
4 stalks celery
4 medium zucchini
2 large onions
2 teaspoons garlic powder
2 tablespoons onion power
12 eggs
1 cup sharp cheddar cheese, shredded
hot sauce to taste
salt to taste
1 prepared deep-dish pie shell

Directions

Preheat oven to 375°.

Chop bell peppers, celery, and onions and sauté in garlic and onion powder. Add salt and hot sauce to taste.

Boil zucchini, drain liquid, and mash. Drain liquid again, if needed. Add mashed zucchini to sautéed vegetables. Season well.

Add crabmeat and shrimp to the vegetable mixture with additional hot sauce, if needed or to taste. Beat eggs thoroughly and add to mixture. Add shredded cheese and stir.

Pour into pie shell. Bake for 45-50 minutes or until golden brown.

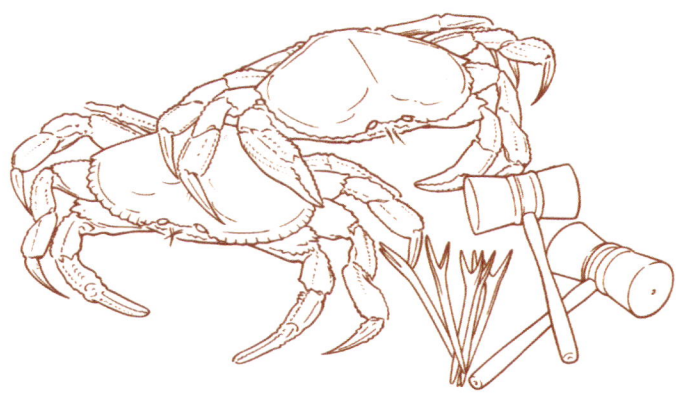

SEVEN SEAS LINGUINI

Contributed by:
Bishop and First Lady Jakes

Number of Servings: 6
Preparation Time: 50 minutes

Ingredients

1 (12 oz.) package linguini
1 cup fat-free butter
fat-free, nonstick cooking spray
2 teaspoons garlic, minced
1/2 cup onion, chopped
12 ounces scallops
12 ounces shrimp, shelled and deveined
12 ounces catfish
12 ounces salmon
12 ounces crab
3 teaspoons herbs
3 teaspoons Sauce Fifth Avenue
4 cups fat-free milk
1 can fat-free evaporated milk
4 teaspoons garlic powder
3 teaspoons cornstarch

Directions

Cook linguini according to package instructions. Rinse with cold water, and drain. Put pasta in a large bowl and mix with a little butter.

Spray skillet with nonstick cooking spray. Sauté garlic and onion over medium heat. Add all seafood, herbs, and Sauce Fifth Avenue and cook until seafood is done.

In a separate saucepan, boil milk and evaporated milk over low heat. Add garlic powder. Mix cornstarch in 1 cup lukewarm water and stir into milk until thickened.

Serve pasta topped with seafood, sauce, and Parmesan cheese, if desired.

LASAGNA

Contributed by:
Pastor Ron Smith

Number of Servings: 6-8
Preparation Time: 1 hour

Ingredients

1 1/2 pounds ground beef
1 onion, chopped
1/2 cup chopped green pepper, optional
1 cup chopped celery, optional
2 cloves garlic, minced
1 tablespoon fresh basil
2 tablespoons parsley
1/2 teaspoon rosemary
1/4 pound sautéed mushrooms, optional
2 tablespoons brown sugar
1 1/2 teaspoons salt
1 (29 oz.) can diced tomatoes or large can Italian tomatoes
2 (6 oz.) cans tomato paste
12 dry lasagna noodles
2 eggs, beaten
1 pint ricotta cheese
1/2 cup grated Parmesan cheese
1 teaspoon salt
1 pound mozzarella cheese, shredded
2 tablespoons grated Parmesan cheese
1 1/3 cup cottage cheese, optional
1 1/3 cups sour cream, optional
1 (6 oz.) package cream cheese, optional

Directions

In large skillet, brown ground beef, celery, green pepper, onion, and garlic over medium heat. Drain fat. Mix in spices, brown sugar, 1 1/2 teaspoons salt, diced tomatoes, and tomato paste. Simmer for 30 to 45 minutes, stirring occasionally. If including mushrooms, in a separate saucepan, sauté mushrooms in 1 tablespoon of butter and them add to mixture.

Preheat oven to 375°. Bring a large pot of lightly salted water to a boil. Add lasagna noodles, cook for 5 to 8 minutes, drain, lay noodles flat on towels, and blot dry.

In a medium bowl, mix together eggs, ricotta, Parmesan cheese, parsley and 1 teaspoon salt. Layer one third of the lasagna noodles in bottom of 9 x 13 baking dish. Cover noodles with half of ricotta mixture, and then half the mozzarella cheese.

If adding the optional cheeses, combine cream cheese, sour cream, and cottage cheese in a mixer and blend well. Spread half of the cream cheese mixture on top of the mozzarella and follow with one third of the sauce. Repeat layering steps, topping with remaining noodles and sauce. Sprinkle additional Parmesan cheese over top.

Bake in preheated oven for 30 minutes. Let stand 10 minutes before serving.

Note: For enhanced flavor, lasagna can be prepared 24 hours in advance and chilled overnight in the refrigerator. Warm and serve.

VEGETABLE LASAGNA

Contributed by:
Bishop and First Lady Jakes

Number of Servings: 4
Preparation Time: 50 minutes

Ingredients

1 (16 oz.) package lasagna noodles
1 zucchini, diced
1 squash, diced
2 cups mushrooms, sliced
1 eggplant, diced
2 teaspoons Italian herbs
2 teaspoons Sauce Fifth Avenue
2 teaspoons garlic powder
fat-free, nonstick cooking spray
4 cups fat-free grated cheese
1 (26 oz.) jar fat-free pasta sauce

Directions

Preheat oven to 300°. Cook pasta according to package directions. Rinse cooked noodles with cold water, drain, and set aside.

Steam vegetables. Put in a large bowl and season with herbs, Sauce Fifth Avenue, and garlic. Spray lasagna pan with fat-free, nonstick cooking spray and place one layer of lasagna noodles on bottom, then a layer of vegetables, followed by a layer of cheese, and then sauce. Repeat until ingredients are gone.

Cover lasagna with aluminum foil and bake for 20 minutes.

JA NAI'S RED SNAPPER WITH PINEAPPLE SALSA

JA NAI'S RED SNAPPER WITH PINEAPPLE SALSA

Contributed by:
Bishop and First Lady Jakes

Number of Servings: 4
Preparation Time: 20 minutes

Ingredients

4 (6 oz.) Red Snapper filets
2 tablespoons olive oil
salt and pepper to taste
1 cup Pineapple Salsa

DIRECTIONS

Season snapper filets with salt and pepper. Heat sauté pan with olive oil over medium heat, and pan sear each side for two minutes. Remove snapper filet from pan and top with pineapple salsa. Serve immediately.

PINEAPPLE SALSA

Ingredients

2 cups fresh pineapple, diced
1/2 cup tomatoes, diced
1/4 cup red onion, diced
1/2 teaspoon jalapeno, diced
1/4 cup cilantro, chopped
juice of 1 lime
salt and pepper to taste

DIRECTIONS

Mix together all ingredients except cilantro, in a large bowl. Pour into serving bowl and fold in cilantro to finish

"*Carefully,* mix all your ingredients together with love. Stir the pot with compassion and understanding, and season the mix with support, encouragement, and respect. The result will surely be a remarkable feast-featuring a variety of gifts and blessings."

FRIENDS AND CELEBRITIES

FISH GRAVY

Contributed by:
Pastor Ghandi

Number of Servings: 6-8
Preparation Time: 45 minutes

Ingredients

5 medium Croaker fish, or other favorite fish
2 medium onions
3 tomatoes
1 small can tomato paste
1/2 cup vegetable oil
1 green bell pepper
red pepper to taste
salt to taste

Directions

Wash and clean fish and cut each fish into 2 pieces. In a large frying pan, fry all of the fish in vegetable oil.

Meanwhile, slice the onions, tomatoes, and bell pepper. Remove fried fish and wash the frying pan. Add 1/2 cup of vegetable oil into the cleaned frying pan, heat oil and add sliced onions. Cook until onions begin to soften, stirring frequently, and add red pepper to taste.

Add sliced tomatoes, pepper, and tomato paste. Stir mixture frequently while it cooks. After the vegetables have cooked down and sauce has thickened slightly, add the fried fish and a little water to the mixture, stirring very carefully. Serve with cooked rice, or boiled yams.

CHILEAN SEA BASS WITH SHRIMP

Contributed by:
Bishop and First Lady Jakes

Number of Servings: 2
Preparation Time: 20 minutes

Ingredients

2 Chilean sea bass steaks
4 jumbo shrimp, deveined
2 cups fresh spinach, chopped
1/2 tablespoon Cajun seasoning
4 tablespoons olive oil
1/2 cup mango sauce (see recipe)
1/2 lemon

Directions

Cut sea bass into 1/2 inch thick square pieces. Heat oil in sauté pan over medium-high heat. Season sea bass and shrimp with Cajun seasoning. Place sea bass in hot sauté pan and pan sear for 2 minutes on both sides. Remove from pan.

Add fresh spinach to a sauté pan and cook briefly or until wilted. In a separate pan, sauté shrimp for 2-3 minutes or until done (shrimp will be pinkish in color). Cut sea bass in half lengthwise and serve on a bed of spinach. Cut cooked shrimp in half, tail off and place pieces in four clockwise positions: 3, 6, 9, and 12. Drizzle mango sauce over entire plate to decorate and serve immediately.

MANGO SAUCE

Ingredients

2 medium yellow ripe mangos
1/4 teaspoon ginger, minced
1/2 cup water
1 cup granulated sugar
1 1/4 teaspoon pure vanilla extract

Directions

Peel and dice mango. Place diced mango in a medium saucepan with all ingredients and bring to a boil. When boiling has started and reaches it's high point, reduce heat and allow the ingredients to simmer on low for an hour. Pour mixture in a blender and puree to finish.

FRIENDS AND CELEBRITIES

DAWN'S DYNAMITE GUMBO

Contributed by:
Dawn Lewis

Number of Servings: 8-12
Preparation Time: 1 hour

Ingredients

1 (14.5 oz.) can chicken broth
1 (14.5 oz.) can seasoned stewed tomatoes
1 small bay leaf
1 tablespoon dried thyme leaves
2 tablespoons butter or margarine
1 cup chopped onions
3/4 cup chopped green peppers
1 tablespoon minced parsley
3 tablespoons file powder (or more according to taste)
3 tablespoons Cajun seasoning
seasoned salt
garlic powder
1 pound diced chicken breast
1 large smoked turkey sausage, sliced
2 cups fresh baby shrimp
2 cups shredded crabmeat
2 cups frozen sliced okra
2 (14 oz.) cans water chestnuts
3 cups cooked rice
hot pepper sauce (optional)

Directions

Separate the chicken and shrimp into a shallow skillet and season with half of the Cajun spices, and grill over low heat until evenly seasoned. Set aside.

Combine chicken broth, tomatoes, water, bay leaf, thyme, butter, onion, green pepper, Cajun seasoning and garlic powder in stockpot or large Dutch oven. Add or subtract spices according to taste for more mild or hot flavoring. Cook 30 minutes.

Add okra. Cook approximately 8-10 minutes. Add the turkey sausage, crabmeat, water chestnuts, and shrimp and chicken mixture, and cook an additional 10 minutes. Let stand 5 minutes. Remove bay leaf before serving.

Cook rice separately and pour the gumbo over it. Season with hot pepper sauce, if desired.

RUSSIAN CHICKEN

Contributed by:
Emmitt and Pat Smith

Number of Servings: 4-6
Preparation Time: 30 minutes

Ingredients

15 to 20 pieces of chicken
garlic salt
seasoning salt
pepper
1/2 cup honey
1/4 cup sugar
4 to 5 bottles of Russian salad dressing

DIRECTIONS

Preheat oven to 425°. Season chicken to taste with garlic salt, pepper, and seasoning salt. Bake chicken covered until done. Drain fat and juices from the pan.

In a separate saucepan, combine the 4 to 5 bottles of dressing, 1/2 cup of honey, and 1/4 cup of sugar and heat for 5 minutes. Pour dressing mixture over chicken and bake an additional 10 to 15 minutes. For added flavor, mushrooms can be added.

FRIENDS AND CELEBRITIES

STUFFED SHRIMP

Contributed by:
Bishop and First Lady Jakes

Number of Servings: 2-4
Preparation Time: 45 minutes

Ingredients

8 jumbo shrimp, deveined
1 1/2 yucca
4 cups seasoned bread crumbs
2 cups flour
1/2 cup cornstarch
3 cups water
vegetable oil for frying
salt and pepper to taste

Directions

Peel and boil yucca until fork-tender. Mash and add salt and pepper to taste. In a small bowl, mix flour, cornstarch, and water until it has a paste-like consistency. In a separate bowl pour in seasoned breadcrumbs.

Butterfly the shrimp. Stuff each shrimp with the mashed yucca and dip into paste mixture. Dip the battered shrimp into the seasoned breadcrumbs. Allow shrimp to sit for 15-30 minutes on a dry baking sheet in the refrigerator.

Heat oil to 300°. Deep fry stuffed shrimp until golden brown. Serve immediately.

SALMON STIR-FRY WITH SAUTÉED VEGETABLES

Submitted by:
Bishop Andrew and First Lady Viveca Merritt

Number of Servings: 6-8
Preparation Time: 40 minutes

Ingredients

1/2 fresh filet Alaskan salmon
1 tablespoon fresh squeezed lemon juice
1-2 tablespoons organic tamari sauce
2 cloves garlic, minced
1/2 cup extra virgin olive oil
1/2 cup onion, finely diced
1 teaspoon seasoning salt, or to taste
1/8 teaspoon cayenne red pepper, or to taste
1/4 cup extra virgin olive oil
1/2 teaspoon seasoning salt
1/2 teaspoon curry powder
1 teaspoon cumin
1/2 cup mushrooms, sliced and diced
1/2 cup celery, sliced
1/2 cup sweet potato, grated
1 cup broccoli spears
1/4 cup peapods
1/2 cup bean sprouts
3 teaspoons low sodium soy sauce, or more to taste
brown rice, prepared according to package directions

Directions

Rinse salmon filet, pat dry, slice down the middle, and cut into chunks. Add lemon juice, tamari sauce, minced garlic, and seasoning salt. Toss all together and set aside.

In a skillet or sauté pan, add 1/2 cup olive oil, onion, and cayenne pepper. Sauté for 2 minutes and add seasoned salmon. Stir-fry until done or for about 5 minutes. Transfer to another dish and set aside.

In the same skillet or sauté pan, heat 1/4 cup olive oil. Add seasoning salt, curry, and cumin. Next add vegetables in the order listed, frying for 1 minute before adding the next vegetable. Finish sautéing all together for approximately 3 minutes. Stir in the soy sauce at the end.

Serve vegetables over brown rice and top with the salmon stir-fry.

ROASTED RACK OF LAMB

Contributed by:
Bishop Eddie and First Lady Vanessa Long

Number of Servings: 4-6
Preparation Time: 30 minutes

Ingredients

1 rack of lamb, frenched (2 each)
3 tablespoons fresh rosemary, minced
3 tablespoons fresh thyme, minced
3 tablespoons fresh basil, minced
4-6 cloves garlic, minced
1 teaspoon salt, or to taste
1 teaspoon pepper
2 tablespoons Dijon mustard
1/2 cup olive oil

DIRECTIONS

Preheat oven to 350°. Drizzle 3-4 tablespoons of olive oil over lamb, and sprinkle evenly with salt and pepper. In a large frying pan, heat the remaining olive oil over medium heat and pan sear the lamb until browned.

Remove lamb and place in a large roasting pan. Mix together the rosemary, thyme, basil, garlic, and Dijon mustard. Firmly rub the herb mixture onto the lamb.

Bake in oven until desired doneness is reached.

HONEY GLAZED BBQ GRILLED SALMON

Contributed by:
Bishop and First Lady Jakes

Number of Servings: 4
Preparation Time: 25 minutes

Ingredients

4 (7 oz.) salmon filets
1/2 tablespoon olive oil
1 lemon
salt and pepper to taste

DIRECTIONS

Prepare salmon filets with salt, pepper, and lemon and brush olive oil on both sides of the filets. Set aside until the grill has reached a temperature of 350°. When grill reaches desired temperature, grill salmon on both sides for 3-5 minutes, making sure to mark indentions on both sides of meat.

Plate the salmon and spoon glaze over the top. Optional: Serve julienne fried sweet potatoes as a garnish.

GLAZE

Ingredients

2 cups pure honey
1 cup BBQ sauce of choice
dash of Louisiana hot sauce

DIRECTIONS

Mix until all ingredients are well blended and serve.

FRIENDS AND CELEBRITIES

SOUTH OF THE BORDER
RIB EYE STEAK

Contributed by:
Deion and Pilar Sanders

Number of Servings: 2-4
Preparation Time: 30 minutes

Ingredients

2 (12 oz.) bone-in rib eye steaks
1 cup of dry red wine
3 tablespoons red wine vinegar
1/4 cup Worcestershire sauce
1 tablespoon coarse brown mustard
3 tablespoons minced garlic
1 tablespoon sugar
1 tablespoon course black pepper
1/2 tablespoon chili powder
1 tablespoon course kosher salt
1/2 tablespoon Tabasco sauce

DIRECTIONS

Combine red wine, vinegar, Worcestershire sauce, mustard, garlic, sugar, black pepper, chili powder, salt, and Tabasco in a medium saucepan. Cook for 20 minutes over medium heat, stirring frequently. Remove from heat and cool in the refrigerator, leaving the pan uncovered.

Put rib eyes in a large Ziploc container and pour cooled marinade over the steaks. Marinate in the refrigerator for at least 1 hour, up to overnight. Remove steaks from the bag and grill to desired doneness.

Suggestion: Serve with twice-baked potatoes and broccoli.

ANGEL WINGS

Contributed by:
Bishop and First Lady Jakes

Number of Servings: 2-4
Preparation Time: 30 minutes

Ingredients

8 whole chicken wings
1 teaspoon cayenne pepper
1 tablespoon seasoned salt
1/4 teaspoon granulated garlic
1/4 teaspoon onion power
2 cups pure honey
1 cup BBQ sauce of choice
vegetable oil for frying

DIRECTIONS

Clean and dry chicken wings, and set aside. Mix all dry seasoning except cayenne in a small bowl. Add dry mixture to chicken wings and toss until coated.

Preheat oil to frying temperature of 350°. In a small saucepan heat honey, BBQ sauce, and cayenne pepper. Once oil is heated, fry seasoned chicken wings for 10-15 minutes or until golden brown. Remove chicken wings from fryer, toss immediately in honey BBQ sauce and serve.

FRIENDS AND CELEBRITIES

STUFFED HERB CREAMED FILET MIGNON

Contributed by:
Bishop and First Lady Jakes

Number of Servings: 4
Preparation Time: 1 hour

Ingredients

4 (9 oz.) tenderloin of beef filets
1 (8 oz.) package cream cheese, softened
1 tablespoon fresh basil, chopped
1 tablespoon fresh thyme, chopped
1 tablespoon fresh oregano, chopped
1/2 tablespoon roasted garlic
1 tablespoon shallots, minced
salt and pepper to taste

Directions

Cut a 1/2 inch hole in the middle of each beef filet and season with salt and pepper, set aside. Mix all fresh herbs together only using 1/2 of the roasted garlic and 1 tablespoon of the shallots. In a medium mixing bowl whip cream cheese and fold in the herb mixture. Let stand for 30 minutes.

Preheat grill to 350°. When grill has reached desired temperature, grill filets on each side for 2 minutes.

Spoon the cream cheese mixture in the center of the filets and place in the oven and broil at 400° for 5 minutes or until the meat is crusted golden brown. Remove from heat, and serve the filets immediately with wine sauce.

WINE SAUCE

Ingredients

1 tablespoon shallots, minced
1/2 tablespoon roasted garlic
2 cups wild mushrooms
2 cups beef stock
1 1/2 cup burgundy wine
1 tablespoon butter

Directions

In a medium saucepan over medium heat, cook the shallots, roasted garlic, 1 cup of beef stock, 1 cup of wild mushrooms, and burgundy wine until reduced. When sauce has reached desired consistency, add remaining mushrooms and beef stock. Cook for 5 more minutes and remove from heat, whisking in the butter. Serve immediately.

CHEESY TURKEY TETRAZZINI

Contributed by:
Issac Hayes

Number of Servings: 6-8
Preparation Time: 45 minutes

Ingredients

8 ounces spaghetti
1 1/2 pounds cooked turkey, diced
2 tablespoons chopped pimientos
1/2 teaspoon chopped fresh parsley
4 tablespoons butter
1/2 cup finely chopped onion
1/4 cup sliced mushrooms
1/4 cup all purpose flour
2 cups milk
1 cup chicken broth
1/4 cup dry sherry
dash of salt
dash of ground white pepper
8 ounces sharp cheddar cheese, shredded

Directions

Preheat oven to 350°. Grease a 3-quart baking dish and set aside.

Cook spaghetti according to package directions. Drain and place in a large bowl. Add the turkey, pimientos, and parsley.

In a medium skillet, melt the butter over medium heat and sauté the onion and mushrooms until softened, about 5 minutes. Blend in the flour and gradually add the milk, chicken broth, and sherry, stirring constantly. Heat to boiling, stirring regularly, over medium-low heat. Simmer until thickened and season with salt and pepper.

Add the sauce to the spaghetti mixture and toss to coat. Spread the mixture into the prepared baking dish and sprinkle cheddar cheese over top.

Bake until heated through and cheese is bubbly, about 35 to 40 minutes.

FRIENDS AND CELEBRITIES

MEXICAN ENCHILADAS

Contributed by:
Co-Pastor Darlene Bishop

Number of Servings: 4-6
Preparation Time: 55 minutes

Ingredients

12 corn tortillas
3-5 tablespoons butter
8 ounces Velveeta Mexican cheese
1/4 cup diced onions
2-3 boneless chicken breasts or
1 pound ground beef
1/2 cup oil
3 tablespoons flour
1 package taco seasoning

DIRECTIONS

Cook meat of choice until done. If using chicken, shred or cut in strips and set aside. If using ground beef, drain excess fat and set aside.

Sauté the tortillas in butter until soft. Fill each tortilla with a wedge of Velveeta cheese, 1 tablespoon of onion, and 3-4 tablespoons of chicken or beef. Roll up tortillas and place seam side down in a baking dish.

Preheat oven to 350°.

In a medium skillet, mix the oil, flour, taco seasoning, and water as needed, cooking over medium heat. Add just enough water to make the sauce the texture of gravy. Pour sauce over tortillas and bake for 10 to 15 minutes.

GRILLED LEMON-LIME CHICKEN

Contributed by:
Pastor Ronnie and Linda Guynes

Number of Servings: 6
Preparation Time: 20 minutes

Ingredients

6 skinless and boneless chicken breast halves
1/2 cup brown sugar
1/3 cup olive oil
1/4 cup apple cider vinegar
3 cloves garlic, crushed
1 tablespoon Dijon mustard
1 1/2 tablespoons lemon juice
1 1/2 tablespoons lime juice
1 1/2 teaspoons salt
1/4 teaspoon pepper

DIRECTIONS

Using the flat side of a mallet, flatten chicken breasts to an approximate thickness of 1/8 inch. Place chicken breasts in a large shallow baking dish and set aside.

Combine the brown sugar, olive oil, vinegar, garlic, mustard, lemon juice, lime juice, salt, and pepper. Stir well and pour over chicken. Cover and refrigerate chicken for two hours.

Remove chicken from marinade and discard marinade. Grill about 4-6 minutes on each side and serve hot.

Serving suggestion: Slice chicken into thin strips and serve with warm tortillas.

FRIENDS AND CELEBRITIES

LUCILLE'S CHILI CHICKEN

Contributed by:
Shirley Murdock

Number of Servings: 6
Preparation Time: 35 minutes

Ingredients

1 package of chicken wings
canola oil
Lawry's seasoning salt
garlic powder
black pepper
flour

Directions

Pour canola oil into a large frying pan, filling approximately half full. Heat canola oil over medium-high heat until really hot. (This is important or the crust will be left in the bottom of the pan.)

While oil is heating, clean chicken wings and season all sides with Lawry's seasoning salt, black pepper, and garlic powder to taste. Dredge the wings in flour, carefully covering all sides.

Once oil is hot, shake off excess flour from the wings, place wings in frying pan, and cover with lid immediately. Every 3 to 4 minutes, lift the lid and turn chicken. Repeat this step until the crust is golden brown.

Remove chicken and drain on paper towels to remove excess oil. Serve hot.

Note: Recommended side dishes are macaroni and cheese, candied yams, collards, and cornbread.

TERESA'S FRIED CATFISH

Contributed by:
Teresa Hairston

Number of Servings: 4-5
Preparation Time: 20 minutes

Ingredients

4-5 fresh catfish filets
1 cup of yellow cornmeal
1 teaspoon salt
1 teaspoon pepper
1 1/2 teaspoons Lawry's seasoning salt
3-4 tablespoons Crisco oil

Directions

Wash filets. In a large freezer bag, combine cornmeal, salt, pepper, and seasoning salt.

Heat Crisco in a heavy cast iron skillet over high heat. Once the oil is very hot, place 2-3 filets at a time in the cornmeal mixture and seal the bag. Shake to thoroughly coat the filets and then place them carefully in the hot oil.

Cook filets on each side about 4-5 minutes or until golden brown. Remove from pan and place on a plate with a paper towel to absorb the excess oil. Serve hot with veggies or favorite side dish.

FRIENDS AND CELEBRITIES

SHEPHERD'S PIE-MEAT LOAF THE SECOND TIME AROUND

Contributed by:
Mrs. Walter Thomas

Number of Servings: 8-10
Preparation Time: 45 minutes

Ingredients

1 1/2 pounds leftover meatloaf
1 cup cooked string beans
2 cups gravy
1 (15 oz.) can mixed vegetables
4 pounds Russet baking potatoes

Directions

Peel and boil potatoes. Drain, cool, and cut into large cubes. Place in a large bowl and set aside.

Mix string beans, mixed vegetables (drain off liquid), and 3 tablespoons of gravy in an 8-inch square baking dish. Stir together and spread in pan evenly. Place in microwave oven and warm for thirty seconds.

Break up meat loaf into bite-sized pieces and place on top of vegetables. Spread remainder of gravy over meatloaf. Heat in microwave for 20 seconds.

Mash the prepared potatoes. Spoon mashed potatoes over entire dish. Heat in microwave for 5 seconds. Serve hot.

Note: Other cooked meats can be substituted for the meatloaf. Be sure to chop or crumble into small pieces.

CHATEAU BRIAND
JUBILEE

Contributed by:
Bishop Sherman S. Watkins

Number of Servings: 4
Preparation Time: 30 minutes

Ingredients

1 full-size Porterhouse Steak, approximately 4 inches thick
unseasoned meat tenderizer
black pepper
vegetable oil
1 can of cherries
orange juice to taste
non-alcoholic red wine
honey or other sweetener

DIRECTIONS

Using a fork, puncture holes in the raw steak on both sides. While holes are still open, fill with unseasoned meat tenderizer and small amounts of black pepper. Use the back of the fork to close up the holes.

Heat a large skillet over high heat. Oil both sides of the steak with vegetable oil and place in the heated skillet. Brown both sides and all edges.

Remove steak from skillet, and cook in the microwave for 8 minutes.

While steak is cooking in the microwave, drain the can of cherries and reserve the juice. In a medium bowl, combine cherry juice with a small amount of regular orange juice to taste. Add wine and mix together with a little honey or sweetener.

Remove the steak from the microwave and coat thoroughly with sauce, letting it drip down the sides of the meat. Garnish with a few cherries and serve hot with the sauce.

DYAN'S COCONUT LEMON GRAHAM CRACKER BARS

Contributed by:
Dyan Cannon

Number of Servings: 6-8
Preparation Time: 20 minutes

Ingredients

1 1/4 cups graham cracker crumbs
1/4 cup sugar
1/3 cup melted butter
2 eggs
1 cup brown sugar, packed
2 tablespoons fresh-squeezed lemon juice
2 teaspoons grated lemon peel
1 1/2 cups shredded coconut
1/2 teaspoon salt

Directions

Preheat oven to 350°. Mix the graham cracker crumbs, sugar, and melted butter thoroughly. Press mixture firmly into the bottom of a square baking dish.

In a separate bowl, beat the eggs well. Add the brown sugar, lemon juice, lemon peel, coconut, and salt. Mix well.

Spread the lemon coconut topping evenly over the graham cracker crust. Bake for 25 minutes, or until topping is golden brown. Cool slightly. Cut into large squares and serve. Excellent chilled as well.

JAMAICAN FRUIT CAKE

Contributed by:
Bishop Noel Jones

Number of Servings: 6-8
Preparation Time: 45 minutes

Ingredients

1 pound butter
1 pound flour
1 pound sugar
1 dozen eggs
8 teaspoons baking power
2 teaspoons cinnamon
1 teaspoon nutmeg
1 pound raisins
1 pound currents
1/4 pound prunes
1/2 pound cherries
1/2 pound mixed citrus peel
2 cups Jamaican white rum, preferably
or (Rum substitute) 2 tablespoons Rum Extract, mixed with 1/2 cup water
4 cups sweet wine
1 bottle browning (Jamaican product)

DIRECTIONS

Three weeks in advance, grind the raisins, currents, prunes, cherries, and citrus peel slightly. Add the rum or the rum substitute, wine, and Browning, and marinate until ready to prepare cake.

Preheat oven to 300°. Cream butter, adding sugar gradually. Then add the eggs, cinnamon, and nutmeg. Mix in the browning fruit mixture, one cup at a time.

Next add flour, one cup at a time, alternating with baking powder. Pour into greased and lined cake pan. Bake until an inserted toothpick comes out clean.

Note: The browning is for color and can be made by cooking 4 ounces of dark sugar in a saucepan over medium heat until liquified and it has a very dark color.

FRIENDS AND CELEBRITIES

STIR-FRIED WILD BERRIES

Contributed by:
Kenny Lattimore

Number of Servings: 5-6
Preparation Time: 20 minutes

Ingredients

5 long stem strawberries
1 cup blackberries
1 cup blueberries
1 cup raspberries
1 cup wine grapes
2 tablespoons brown sugar
1 tablespoon butter
1/2 cup fruit juice of choice
10 chocolate poky sticks

Optional: 1 lemon
Plain or Vanilla Yogurt

Directions

Frost your favorite dessert bowl or individual glasses in the freezer. Mix the berries and grapes in a medium bowl and set aside. In a large saucepan over medium-low heat, melt the butter. Add the brown sugar and stir until it dissolves. Add the berry mixture and cook for 1 minute.

Slowly stir in juice and cook for an additional minute. Carefully spoon berries into frosted dessert bowl or glasses and top with vanilla ice cream and 2 poky sticks.

Optional Variation:

As a substitute for the ice cream, zest and mince 1 lemon and fold into either plain or sweet vanilla yogurt to taste.

MORNING GLORY FRUIT SMOOTHIE

Contributed by:
Thad Bosley

Number of Servings: 2
Preparation Time: 10 minutes

Ingredients

1/2 cup frozen strawberries, sliced
1/2 cup bananas, sliced
1/2 cup of orange juice
1/2 cup raspberry yogurt
5 ice cubes

Directions

Wash strawberries and slice the fruit. Place all ingredients in a blender and puree until smooth.

FRIENDS AND CELEBRITIES

SWEET POTATO PIE

Contributed by:
Beverly Crawford

Number of Servings: 10-12
Preparation Time: 55 minutes

Ingredients

4 sweet potatoes
1 stick butter
3 eggs
1 cup granulated sugar
1/2 cup light brown sugar
1 teaspoon vanilla flavoring
1 teaspoon almond flavoring
1 teaspoon lemon flavoring
1/2 can condensed milk
2 prepared deep pie crusts

Directions

Preheat oven to 350°.

Boil potatoes until soft. Peel potatoes with a fork while still hot, removing all skin. In a large mixing bowl, mash the potatoes until lump-free. Melt butter and pour over potatoes.

Add butter, eggs, granulated and brown sugars, condensed milk, and all flavorings to the mashed potato mixture. Mix well and pour into 2 deep pan crusts. Bake in preheated oven for 1 hour until lightly browned.

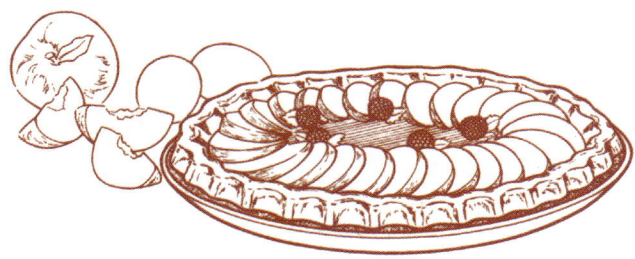

HEAVENLY CHOCOLATE

Contributed by:
Marcus and Joni Lamb

Number of Servings: 8-10
Preparation Time: 40 minutes

Ingredients

1 stick margarine
3/4 cup flour
1/2 cup chopped pecans
1 (8 oz.) package cream cheese, softened
1 cup powdered sugar
1 large container Cool Whip
2 small boxes instant chocolate pudding
3 cups milk

DIRECTIONS

Preheat oven to 350°. Melt margarine in an oblong glass baking dish. Sprinkle in flour and chopped pecans. Bake until golden brown. Remove and cool for approximately 15 minutes.

Combine softened cream cheese, powdered sugar, and 1 cup Cool Whip. Blend well and spread over first layer.

Mix both boxes of instant chocolate pudding with the milk, beating well. Spread evenly over cream cheese layer.

Finally, spread the remaining Cool Whip evenly over top, and serve.

LES BROWN'S VANILLA WAFER CAKE

Contributed by:
Les Brown

Number of Servings: 6-8
Preparation Time: 20 minutes

Ingredients

1 cup butter
2 cups sifted sugar
6 large eggs, separated
1 (12 oz.) package vanilla wafers, rolled fine
1 (7 oz.) package extra moist sweetened coconut
1 cup chopped pecans

Directions

Preheat oven to 350°. Cream the butter and sugar. In a separate small mixing bowl, beat the egg yolks until thickened. Add to creamed butter mixture and blend well.

Add vanilla wafers, coconut, and chopped pecans. In a separate mixing bowl, beat the egg whites and then fold into batter. Mix well.

Spoon batter into a well-greased tube cake pan. Bake for 1 hour and 10 minutes.

FANTASY FUDGE

Contributed by:
Pastor Ron Smith

Number of Servings: 12-15
Preparation Time: 20 minutes

Ingredients

3 cups sugar
3/4 cup butter or margarine
2/3 cup evaporated milk
1 (12 oz.) package semi-sweet chocolate pieces
1 (7 oz.) jar marshmallow crème
1 teaspoon pure vanilla extract
1 cup chopped nuts

Directions

Combine sugar, butter, and evaporated milk in a 2-quart glass bowl. Microwave on high, covered, for 5 minutes or until mixture starts to boil, stirring once.

Microwave on high uncovered, for 5 minutes. Stir in chocolate pieces until smooth. Blend in marshmallow crème and vanilla. Stir in nuts. Pour into greased 12 x 8 inch baking dish. Cool until set and cut into squares. Makes about 3 pounds.

Note: Cooking times may vary with different microwave or combination ovens.

CHOCOLATE ICED CAKE

Contributed by:
Pastor Ronnie and Linda Guynes

Number of Servings: 8-10
Preparation Time: 45 minutes

Ingredients

2 cups all purpose flour
2 cups granulated sugar
3 tablespoons cocoa
1 stick butter
1/2 cup cooking oil
1 cup water
2 eggs
1 teaspoon pure vanilla extract
1/2 cup buttermilk
1 teaspoon baking soda
1 tablespoon cocoa
1 box powdered sugar
7 tablespoons milk
1 teaspoon pure vanilla extract

Directions

Preheat oven to 350°.

In a large mixing bowl, combine sugar and flour. Set aside. In a medium saucepan, combine butter, cooking oil, 3 tablespoons cocoa, and water. Slowly bring to a boil.

Add heated cocoa mixture to the sugar and flour. Add buttermilk, baking soda, eggs, and vanilla and mix well. Spray a 9 x 13 glass or metal baking pan with nonstick cooking spray. Pour batter into baking pan. Bake in preheated oven for 20 minutes. Let cake cool for 10 minutes.

While cake is cooling, in large bowl combine 1 tablespoon cocoa, powdered sugar, milk, and 1 teaspoon vanilla. Mix well until all sugar is dissolved. Poke holes in cake with a fork. Pour icing immediately over cake and serve.

PEACH COBBLER

Contributed by:
Mrs. Mary Sanders

Number of Servings: 6
Preparation Time: 40 minutes

Ingredients

1/4 cup margarine, melted
2 (16 oz.) cans of peaches
3/4 cup flour
2/3 cup sugar
1 teaspoon baking powder
1/4 cup skim milk

DIRECTIONS

Preheat oven to 375°. Coat a 9 inch square baking pan with nonstick cooking spray. Pour in melted margarine and set aside.

Drain peaches, reserving 1/2 cup syrup and set aside.

Combine flour, sugar, and baking powder in a medium bowl. Add peach syrup and skim milk to dry ingredients. Stir until just moist. Pour batter into prepared dish and top with peaches. Do not stir.

Bake for 35 minutes or until golden brown.

FRIENDS AND CELEBRITIES

SPRITE POUND CAKE

Contributed by:
Les Brown

Number of Servings: 8-12
Preparation Time: 25 minutes

Ingredients

3 cups sugar
3 sticks butter
6 eggs
3 cups flour
3/4 cup Sprite
3 teaspoons lemon flavoring

DIRECTIONS

Preheat oven to 325°.

In a large mixing bowl, cream the sugar and butter until smooth. Add one egg at a time and beat thoroughly. Gradually add all of the flour and mix well.

Combine the Sprite and lemon flavoring and mix into batter until smooth, bake in a loaf pan for 1 hour.

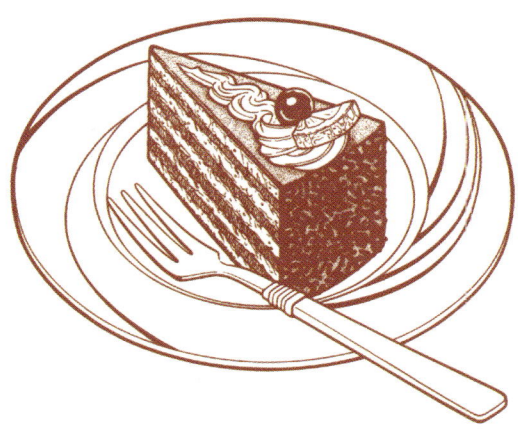

T'S DOWN-HOME APPLE PIE

Contributed by:
Teresa Hairston

Number of Servings: 6
Preparation Time: 1 hour

Ingredients

5-6 medium Granny Smith apples
1 1/3 cups sugar
1 teaspoon lemon juice
1 tablespoon flour
1 tablespoon nutmeg
3 tablespoons butter or margarine
prepared, frozen piecrust

Directions

Preheat oven to 400°. Set out the frozen pie crust to thaw. Once crust is thawed, prepare a pie pan with the bottom crust.

Wash, core, and cut the apples, slicing them to an approximate thickness of 1/8 inch. Place sliced apples in a large mixing bowl and add all of the other ingredients. Stir the mixture carefully and spoon into prepared piecrust.

Cover apples with top crust and pinch the edges to achieve a fluted effect. Trim any excess crust and make a few slits near the top of the crust using a sharp knife, to let the steam escape.

Bake for 50 minutes, watching to make sure the piecrust doesn't brown too quickly. When pie is finished, turn off heat and let the pie sit in the hot oven for another 15-20 minutes.

ZUCCHINI AND SQUASH MEDLEY

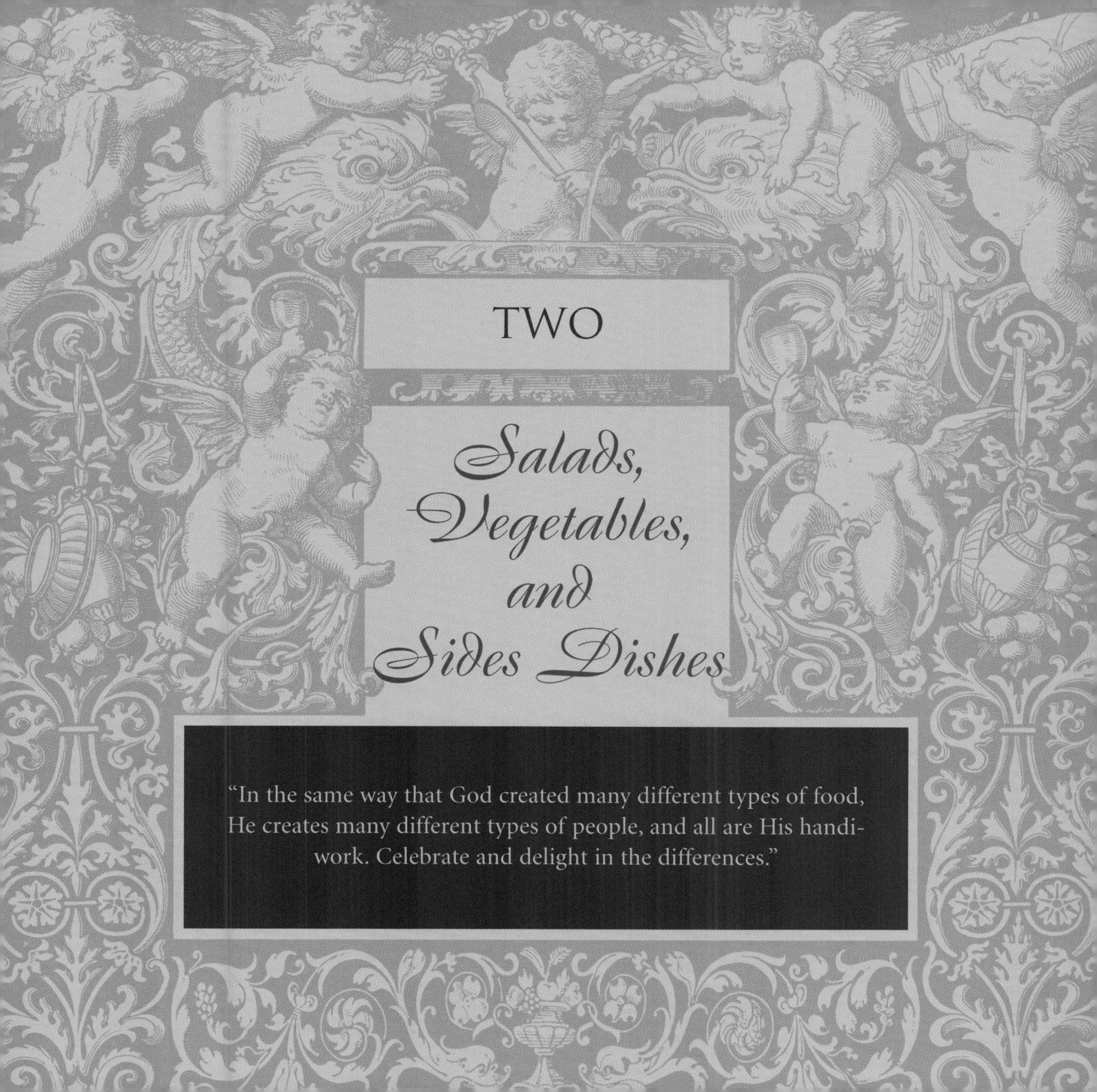

TWO

Salads, Vegetables, and Sides Dishes

"In the same way that God created many different types of food, He creates many different types of people, and all are His handiwork. Celebrate and delight in the differences."

VEGGIE CRAB SALAD

Number of Servings: 6
Preparation Time: 30 minutes

Ingredients

1 head cauliflower
1 bunch broccoli
1 package frozen peas
1 pound crabmeat
1 cup mayonnaise
seasoning salt
garlic salt
Accent salt

Directions

Cut the cauliflower and broccoli into bite-sized pieces, and place in a large salad bowl. Add the frozen peas. Flake the crabmeat into bite-sized pieces and add to the vegetable mixture. Mix in the mayonnaise until lightly coated, either by hand or using a spoon. Season to taste with seasoning salt and Accent. Serve.

IRRESISTIBLE CHINESE CHICKEN SALAD

Ingredients

2 large cooked chicken breasts, shredded
1/2 package won ton skins
3 green onions, thinly chopped
1/2 bunch cilantro, chopped
1 head lettuce or 1 pound fresh salad mix (wash and tear or use fresh salad mix)
1 (4 oz.) can water chestnuts, sliced
3 tablespoons toasted sesame seeds

Directions

Cut the won ton skins into 1/4-inch slices and deep fry in hot vegetable oil. Set fried won tons aside on paper towels to drain fat. (Fried won tons can be purchased at a local Chinese restaurant.) Wash and tear lettuce into bite-sized pieces and add to a large salad bowl. Add the green onions, cilantro, water chestnuts, sesame seeds, and chicken, and mix well. Toss with salad dressing and top with the fried won tons. Serve immediately.

DRESSING

Ingredients

4 tablespoons sugar
1 teaspoon salt
1 teaspoon pepper
1/2 cup salad oil
2 tablespoons sesame oil
6 tablespoons rice vinegar

Directions

Heat ingredients in small sauce pan until sugar is dissolved. (Do not boil.) Cool dressing and toss with salad.

SALADS, VEGETABLES, AND SIDE DISHES

SPINACH SALAD

Number of Servings: 6-8
Preparation Time: 20 minutes

Ingredients

1 large bag fresh spinach, cut
1/2 green bell pepper, thinly sliced
1/2 red bell pepper, thinly sliced
1/2 yellow bell pepper, thinly sliced
7-10 cherry tomatoes cut in halves
3 stems of green onions, chopped
1 small cucumber, thinly sliced
1/8 cup sunflower seeds, toasted
(can substitute 1/4 cup walnuts,
chopped in small pieces)
1/2 sweet red apple, thinly sliced
(can substitute 1/2 cup green seedless
grapes, cut in halves)
1/4 cup raisins (optional)
1 package of cooked, Louis Rich
mesquite grilled chicken breasts
2 boiled eggs, thinly sliced
1 cup garlic and onion croutons
1/8 cup shredded mild cheddar cheese
Mrs. Dash or seasoning of preference
1/2 cup shredded cheese
Ranch salad dressing (optional)

Directions

Combine all ingredients in large bowl. Season with Mrs. Dash to taste, toss gently for coating. Sprinkle top with shredded cheese before serving. Chill for 15-30 minutes and serve.

BROILED TUNA AND RASPBERRY SALAD

Number of Servings: 2
Preparation Time: 25 minutes

Ingredients

1/2 cup Vidalia Onion Vinaigrette dressing
1/4 cup raspberry vinegar
1 1/2 teaspoon Cajun seasoning
1 thick-sliced tuna steak (about 6-8 oz)
3-4 cups wild field greens
1/2 cup fresh raspberries
1/2 cup thinly sliced green onion
2 tablespoon toasted sesame seeds

Directions

Combine salad dressing, vinegar, and Cajun seasoning. Pour 1/4 cup salad dressing mixture into a plastic Ziplock bag to use as a marinade, reserving remaining mixture. Add tuna to marinade. Seal bag and turn to coat tuna. Marinate in the refrigerator 10 minutes, turning once.

Preheat broiler. Spray rack of broiler pan with nonstick cooking spray. Place tuna on rack. Broil tuna, 4 inches from heat for 5 minutes. Turn tuna and brush with marinade; discard remaining marinade. Broil 5 minutes more or until tuna flakes in center. Cool 5 minutes. Cut into 1/4 inch slices.

Toss lettuce mixture together in large bowl; divide evenly between two serving plates. Top with tuna and raspberries; drizzle with reserved salad dressing mixture.

QUEEN SALAD

Number of Servings: 6-8
Preparation Time: 30 minutes

Ingredients

1 can cherry pie filling
1 can Eagle brand milk
1 can crushed pineapple
2 tablespoons concentrated lemon juice
1 small bag chopped pecans
1 container Cool Whip
1 small jar maraschino cherries
Optional: 1 prepared graham cracker crust

Directions

Completely drain the crushed pineapple. Empty can into a large bowl and mix with Eagle brand milk, pie filling, and half of the chopped pecans.

Gently fold in the Cool Whip until it becomes red. If desired, pour mixture into a graham cracker crust. Otherwise, salad can be served directly from mixing bowl. Sprinkle the remainder of the chopped pecans on top and decorate with maraschino cherries. Chill for 15-30 minutes and serve.

SPICY ARTICHOKE, BABY SHRIMP, AND ORZO SALAD

Number of Servings: 4
Preparation Time: 30 minutes

Ingredients

2 1/2 quarts water
1/3 cup fresh lemon juice
1 pound cooked shrimp (optional)
1 medium size jar marinated artichoke hearts (use as many as desired, but not less than 8)
1/2 pound orzo or other rice shape pasta
2 tablespoons olive oil (may use the canned artichoke marinade)
1/4 cup red bell pepper, roasted, peeled, and diced
1/4 cup diced sweet onion
1/4 cup diced celery
1 seeded jalapeno pepper
2 tablespoons Dijon mustard
2 tablespoons chopped fresh tarragon, cilantro or parsley, or 1/2 teaspoon dried Lawry's Seasoning Salt and Seasoned Pepper

DIRECTIONS

Combine the water and lemon juice in a large saucepan and bring to boil over high heat. Cook the orzo until it is al dente (tender but firm to the bite).

Take 6-8 artichokes and mix with orzo in a large bowl. Add the olive oil or artichoke marinade and, with a fork, toss to coat evenly.

In a small bowl, combine the roasted peppers, diced onions, jalapeno pepper, celery, mustard, vinegar, fresh or dried herbs, and the cooked shrimp. Stir to mix well. Add to the orzo mixture and toss to coat the ingredients evenly. Flavor with Lawry's Seasoning Salt and Seasoned Pepper to taste.

SALADS, VEGETABLES, AND SIDE DISHES

PASTA SALAD

Number of Servings: 8
Preparation Time: 25 minutes

Ingredients

1 (12 oz.) package tri-color curly pasta
1 teaspoon salt
1/2 cup chopped sweet red onions
1/2 cup red pepper, julienne
1/2 cup green bell pepper, julienne
1/2 cup chopped celery
1/2 cup black olives, quartered
1/2 cup green olives
1 cup Vidalia sweet onion vinaigrette dressing
1/4 cup Italian dressing
Lawry's Seasoning Salt
Lawry's Salt-Free 17 seasoning
black pepper

Directions

Cook pasta according to package directions, adding 1 teaspoon of salt to water. Rinse pasta in cold water and let drain. Add celery, onions, olives, and bell peppers. Add vinaigrette and Italian dressing. Season to taste with Lawry's Seasoning Salt, Lawry's Salt-Free 17 seasoning, and black pepper.

SAM'S CHILI SAUCE

Number of Servings: 20
Preparation Time: 15 minutes

Ingredients

1/2 cup chili blend
1/2 cup ground cumin
1/4 cup sugar
1 - 1 1/2 cups vinegar
1/4 teaspoon red pepper

Directions

Combine all ingredients together in a medium bowl. Make sure it forms a thick liquid by varying the amount of vinegar to the desired consistency. Allow the sauce to blend together at least overnight to develop the best flavor. If desired, increase the amount of red pepper to taste for a hotter sauce.

SALADS, VEGETABLES, AND SIDE DISHES

SAM'S PICANTE SAUCE

Number of Servings: 20
Preparation Time: 15 minutes

Ingredients

1/4 cup onions, chopped
1/4 cup bell pepper, chopped
2 teaspoons cilantro, chopped
1 teaspoon celery, finely chopped
1 (16 oz. can) tomato sauce
1 teaspoon jalapeno pepper, chopped
1 teaspoon lemon juice
1 1/2 teaspoons sugar

Directions

Combine all ingredients in a medium saucepan and slowly cook over medium heat. Refrigerate overnight and serve with chips or any with food that requires picante sauce.

SEAFOOD DIP

Number of Servings: 6-8
Preparation Time: 20 minutes

Ingredients

1 (12 oz.) jar seafood cocktail sauce
1 (8 oz.) package cream cheese
1 cup sour cream
1/3 cup mayonnaise
1/2 pound shredded cheese
1 large green pepper, diced
1 large red pepper, diced
1 large tomato, diced

Directions

Using an electric mixer, blend cream cheese, mayonnaise, and sour cream until smooth.

In the bottom of an 8 oz. round glass dish, evenly spread the cream cheese mixture. Cover with a layer of seafood cocktail sauce, followed by the shredded cheese. Top with a layer of the green pepper, red pepper, and tomato.

SALADS, VEGETABLES, AND SIDE DISHES

JOAN'S GREENS WITHOUT MEAT

Number of Servings: 6-8
Preparation Time: 45 minutes

Ingredients

6 bunches of fresh greens (any single type or combination of collards, mustard, or turnips)
1 medium red onion, sliced or cut into strips
1 medium yellow onion, sliced or cut into strips
1 clove garlic, whole or minced
1 bell pepper, diced
Frank's Louisiana hot sauce
1 stick butter

Directions

Prepare greens by washing and cutting. Set them aside. Melt the butter in a saucepan and sauté the onions, bell pepper, and minced garlic until lightly brown. (If using whole garlic, add later.)

Fill a large pot with approximately 1 quart of water, add half of the sautéed vegetables and all of the greens. Top with the remaining vegetables and cook on high for 1 hour. (Whole garlic may be added now.) Reduce heat and continue to cook for approximately 2 more hours. Season with the hot sauce to taste and cook for 1 more hour. (Note: add water if needed.) Add additional hot sauce as needed.

GLORIOUS GREENS, GLORIOUS GREENS

Number of Servings: 6-8
Preparation Time: 2 1/2 hours

Ingredients

4-5 bunches collard greens
1 package smoked turkey wings
crushed red pepper
1 onion
2 tomatoes
6-10 pepperoni slices
hot sauce

Directions

Clean and prepare greens. Dice turkey wings and sauté in a frying pan. In a four quart pot, fill 1/3 full of water. Add collard greens, crushed red pepper, sautéed turkey wings, and drippings, and bring to a boil. Simmer collards on low for approximately 1 1/2 hours. Add optional topping and serve.

Optional: Chop onions, pepperoni, and tomatoes. Chill and serve over collards with hot sauce

SALADS, VEGETABLES, AND SIDE DISHES

VEGETABLE SUCCOTASH

Number of Servings: 6-8
Preparation Time: 30 minutes

Ingredients

fat back
1 pound field peas with snaps,
1 pound green lima beans,
1/2 pound mixed vegetables,
2 cloves garlic
1 (15 1/2 oz.) can whole kernel corn
1 (14 1/2 oz.) can stewed tomatoes
garlic salt
black pepper

Directions

Fry 4 pieces of fat back in a stew pot. Remove the fat back, drain, and discard the grease. In the same pot, crumble the fried fat back. Add the field peas, green lima beans, and the additional mixed vegetables. Place just enough water to cover the vegetables and boil over medium heat. Crush 2 cloves of garlic and add to boiling stew.

Add the kernel corn, stewed tomatoes, garlic salt, and black pepper to taste. Cook vegetables to desired consistency. Serve over white rice with rolls.

EASY FRIED CABBAGE

Number of Servings: 6-8
Preparation Time: 30-45 minutes

Ingredients

1 head cabbage, shredded
1 small onion
1 clove garlic
1 bell pepper
4 slices bacon
1 tablespoon vinegar, optional

Directions

Cut up bacon into small pieces and brown in large frying pan. Chop onion, garlic, and bell pepper, add to bacon and stir. Add cabbage and vinegar. Cover frying pan and cook over low heat, stirring often, until desired tenderness. Serve with cornbread.

SALADS, VEGETABLES, AND SIDE DISHES

ZUCCHINI AND SQUASH MEDLEY

Number of Servings: 6-8
Preparation Time: 20 minutes

Ingredients

3 medium zucchini
3 medium yellow squash
2 tablespoons olive oil
1 can Del Monte diced herbed tomatoes
fresh basil
1/2 cup freshly grated Parmesan cheese
salt & pepper to taste

Directions

Cut zucchini and squash into 1/4 inch thick slices. Heat olive oil in sauté pan over medium heat and sauté vegetables until al dente. Stir in diced tomatoes and mix well. Remove from heat and spoon into a serving dish. Sprinkle top with Parmesan cheese and garnish with fresh basil.

SALADS, VEGETABLES, AND SIDE DISHES

SELAH QUICHE

Number of Servings: 6
Preparation Time: 50 minutes

Ingredients

9 1/2 inch quiche pan or pie shell
3 oz. Swiss cheese, sliced or grated
2 oz. sharp cheddar cheese
1 (6 1/2 oz.) container crabmeat
7 jumbo shrimp, whole or diced
3 eggs, beaten
1 cup whipping cream, heated
2 whole fresh mushrooms
1/4 of one onion, diced
1/2 teaspoon grated lemon peel
1/2 teaspoon salt
1/2 teaspoon whole pepper
1/2 teaspoon dry mustard
pinch of fresh basil
1/4 cup slivered almonds

Directions

Bake pie shell for 10 minutes at 450°. Cool pie shell slightly, and sprinkle cheese, onions, and mushrooms over bottom crust. Top with shrimp and crabmeat. Beat eggs thoroughly and mix with heated whipping cream, salt, pepper, and dry mustard. Pour egg mixture over the cheese and seafood, let stand for 10 minutes.

Sprinkle with nutmeg, and top with slivered almonds before baking. Bake at 350° for 35-45 minutes. Remove, let stand for 10 minutes before serving.

MORY'S FRITTATA

Number of Servings: 4 to 6
Preparation Time:

Ingredients

1 pound homemade turkey sausage or Polish K
1/2 green pepper
1 small white onion
1 rib celery
2 cloves garlic
6 eggs
1/4 cup cream plus 2 tablespoons water
1 cup broccoli or string beans or asparagus
1/2 cup grated cheese
1/4 cup grated sharp cheese

Directions

Steam chosen vegetable for 6 minutes and set aside. In a large nonstick frying pan cook sausage until almost done. Chop pepper, onion, celery, and garlic and add to sausage.

In a medium mixing bowl, beat eggs with cream and water mixture. Pour egg mixture over sausage in frying pan. Add salt & pepper to taste.

Sprinkle 1/2 cheese on top and arrange steamed vegetable on top. Push gently towards center, as in making an omelet, cover and cook for 8 to 10 minutes. Sprinkle the remainder of cheese on top and put under broiler until cheese melts.

Serve with fresh fruit or sliced tomatoes.

CHEESE AND CORN PUDDING

Number of Servings: 4-6
Preparation Time: 30 minutes

Ingredients

3 eggs
3 tablespoons flour
1/2 cup cream
1 cup milk
dash of nutmeg
1/2 teaspoon salt
1/4 teaspoon pepper
pinch of sugar
2 cups corn
4 tablespoons melted butter
1/2 cup grated cheese (sharp and cheddar mixed)

Directions

Preheat oven to 350°. Beat eggs and flour together. Add cream, milk, salt, pepper, nutmeg, and sugar. Mix in corn and butter. Thoroughly mix ingredients.

Butter a medium-sized casserole dish. Pour in corn mixture. Place casserole into a larger pan, filled halfway with water.

Bake for 55 minutes to 1 hour.

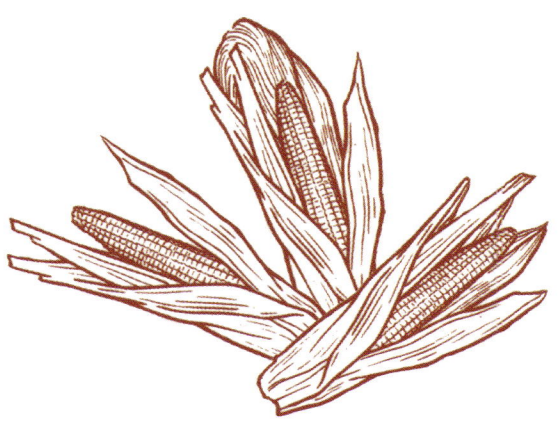

NEW ORLEANS RED BEANS AND RICE

Number of Servings: 5-8
Preparation Time: 30 minutes

Ingredients

1 pound red kidney beans
1 medium white onion
1 teaspoon cayenne pepper
2 tablespoons Creole seasoning salt
1 to 2 pounds smoked turkey necks and/or wings
1 pound beef smoked sausage (optional)
salt & pepper to taste

Directions

Soak dried beans in water for 1 hour. Drain water and remove any damaged beans. Combine all remaining ingredients in a large soup pot. Add 4-6 cups of water. Simmer on low heat for 1 1/2 hours or until beans are soft. To make red beans creamier, smash the cooked beans against the side of the pot or add 1 teaspoon of cooking oil. Serve over rice.

> "*Regardless* of who comprises your family unit, the most important thing is that your family is a mutually supportive entity that shares common goals and aspirations."
>
> —Bishop T.D. Jakes

SALADS, VEGETABLES, AND SIDE DISHES

CRAZY BEANS

Number of Servings: 6-8
Preparation Time: 45 minutes

Ingredients

2 pounds ground sirloin
1 cup onion, diced
1/4 cup bell pepper, chopped
1 (8 oz.) can tomato sauce
1 (14.5 oz.) can stewed tomatoes
1 (52 oz.) can Ranch Style Beans
1 (15 oz.) can Ranch Style Kidney Beans, optional
1 (15 oz.) can Ranch Style Black Beans, optional
1 (15 oz.) can Wolf Brand Chili
seasoning salt
garlic salt
black pepper
Tabasco sauce

Directions

In a large skillet, brown 2 pounds ground sirloin, or preferred ground meat, with diced onion and chopped bell pepper. Add seasoning salt, garlic salt, and black pepper to taste.

Add tomato sauce and 2 cans of water. Add stewed tomatoes and cook slowly. Heat Ranch Style Beans in a large pot over medium heat. To make it crazy, add kidney and black beans (optional). Stir in Wolf Brand Chili. Heat until ready. Stir in cooked meat for the last 15 minutes of cooking. Add a splash of Tabasco pepper sauce to taste.

LOUISIANA CAJUN STYLE
DIRTY RICE

Number of Servings: 6-12
Preparation Time: 1 hour

Ingredients

1-2 pounds pure ground beef
1 small yellow onion
1/2 small green bell pepper
1 teaspoon oregano
1 tablespoon dry crushed red pepper
2 teaspoons garlic salt
1/2 cup parsley flakes
1 teaspoon black pepper
3 teaspoons Cajun seasoning
Uncle Ben's Whole Grain White Rice

Directions

Dice yellow onion, and brown in a large skillet with ground beef. Drain off excess grease. Slice green bell pepper into thin strips and add to beef mixture. Cook over medium heat and sprinkle in parsley flakes, black pepper, oregano, garlic salt, Cajun seasoning, and dry crushed red pepper. Mix thoroughly.

Add 2 cups of Uncle Ben's Whole Grain rice and 3 1/2 cups of water. Bring all ingredients to a boil. Stir occasionally to distribute seasoning evenly and avoid sticking. As the water starts to dissipate, lower heat and cover skillet. Simmer for 15-20 minutes. Sprinkle 1/2 teaspoon crushed pepper over top and serve.

SALADS, VEGETABLES, AND SIDE DISHES

CHILEAN SEA BASS WITH SHRIMP

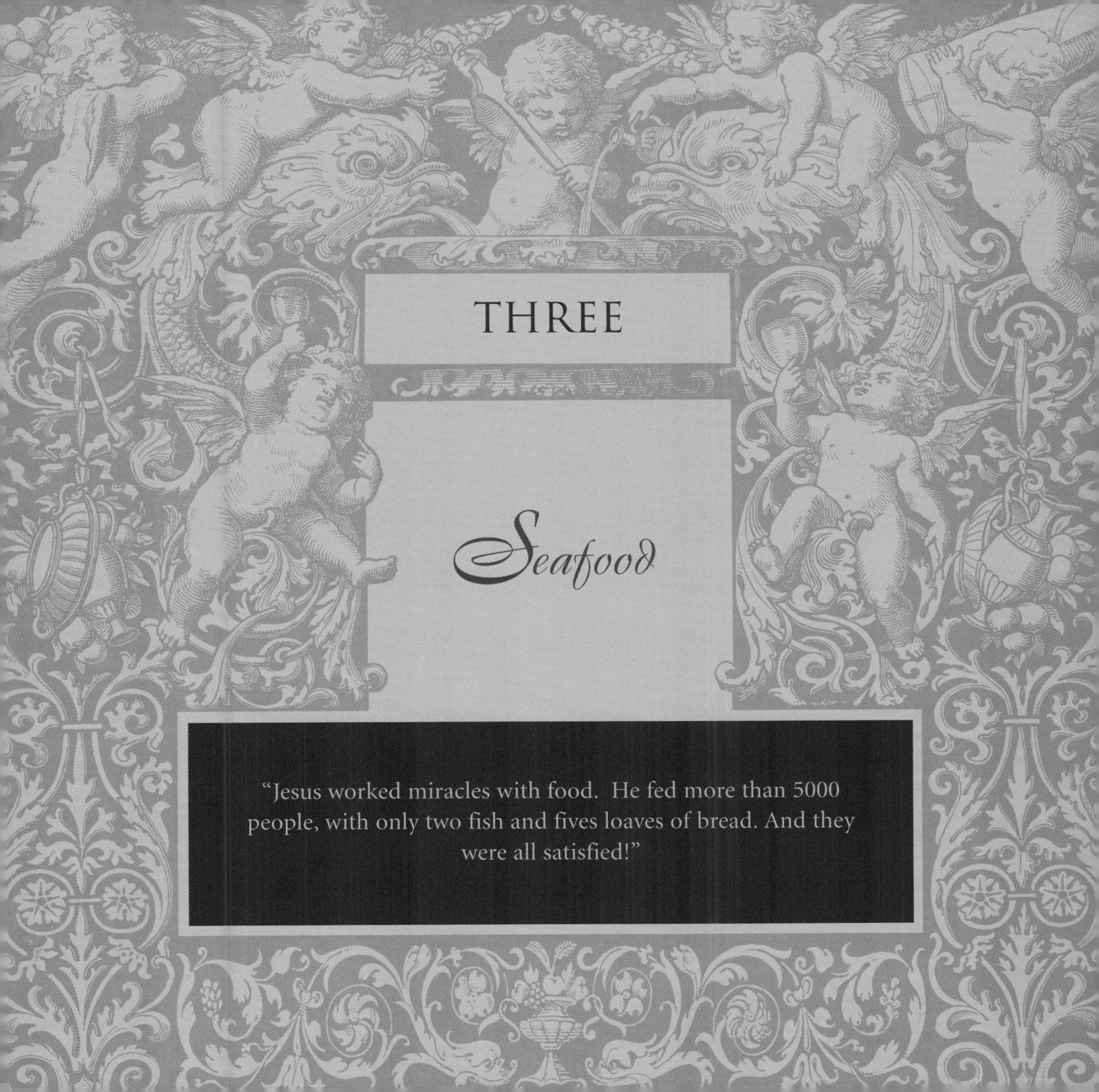

THREE

Seafood

"Jesus worked miracles with food. He fed more than 5000 people, with only two fish and fives loaves of bread. And they were all satisfied!"

BARBECUE SHRIMP

Number of Servings: 6
Preparation Time: 30 minutes

Ingredients

5 pounds fresh shrimp with shells
1 stick margarine
1 chopped onion
1 tablespoon chopped garlic
parsley to taste
Tony Chachere's Creole Seasoning, to taste
Italian bread crumbs to taste

Directions

Wash shrimp and remove heads. Put shrimp into pot. Do not add water. Add margarine, onion, garlic, and parsley, and cook over medium heat. Add breadcrumbs and Creole Seasoning to mixture. Stir shrimp until they turn pink (when you are sure they are done). Add additional Creole seasoning, if needed. Serve with garlic bread and extra sauce for dipping.

STUFFED SHRIMP

FRIENDS AND CELEBRITIES

EXOTIC SOUTHERN STYLE
GUMBO

Number of Servings: 8-10
Preparation Time: 2 hours

Ingredients

2 cups crabmeat
3 pounds shrimp, in shells
3 quarts water
2 bay leaves
1 lemon, sliced
1 package shrimp boil
salt, red pepper, and black pepper
parsley
2 pounds okra, sliced
6 tablespoons bacon grease, divided
4 tomatoes, peeled and chopped
2 pounds Thomasville sausage, cut in 1/2 inch pieces
2 pounds boneless chicken breasts, cubed
3 lobster tails, in shell
2 onions, finely chopped
2 green peppers, finely chopped
2 red peppers, finely chopped

Directions

Make the roux first. The fat used for the roux may be oil, shortening, bacon drippings, or butter. Combine fat with an equal amount of flour. 1/2 cup of each will make plenty.

Melt the fat in a black skillet over low heat. When warm and fluid, add the flour a little at a time while stirring. Stir constantly until brown (this may take 20-30 minutes). Immediately remove from heat and set aside. (If it burns, evenly slightly, throw it out and start over again.)

In a large Dutch oven, boil the water with bay leaves, lemon, 2 slices of onion, salt, pepper, red pepper, and parsley. Wash lobster tails and add to pot. Boil for 15 minutes. Wash shrimp and boil for 2 minutes. Peel lobster tails and shrimp and return shells to stock for later use. Set lobster tails, shrimp and crabmeat aside. Boil chicken pieces in stock for 15 minutes and set chicken with lobster tails, shrimp, and crabmeat.

Sauté okra slices in three tablespoons bacon grease in large black skillet. When soft, transfer to a stew pot and add tomatoes (Rotel and Del Monte) along with cut up Thomasville sausage. Stir and mix together well. Clean skillet and add 3 remaining tablespoons bacon grease to it. Sauté the finely chopped onions, and green and red peppers. When soft, add these ingredients to the stew pot.

4 tablespoons brown roux
1 tablespoon gumbo file
reserved shrimp stock
salt, pepper, thyme, and parsley,
to taste
1 can Rotel tomatoes
1 can Del Monte Diced Tomatoes with
Basil & Oregano
Garlic
hot boiled rice

In saucepan warm the roux. Strain and stir in 2 cups of the shrimp stock. When well blended, add to the large stew pot with the other ingredients. Bring to a boil and simmer for 2 hours, adding more strained stock if needed for consistency. Adjust seasonings with the salt, pepper, thyme, and parsley. When it has simmered for at least 3-4 hours and the flavors have begun to blend, add the shrimp, lobster tails (cut up), chicken, and crabmeat. Cook for 15 more minutes. Serve with fresh boiled rice.

SHRIMP PRIMAVERA

SHRIMP PRIMAVERA

Number of Servings: 4-6
Preparation Time: 1 hour

Ingredients

1/2 pound shrimp, peeled and deveined
1 cup heavy cream
1/2 cup chopped celery
1/4 cup diced onion
1/2 cup diced raw carrots
1 cup diced Roma tomatoes
1/2 tablespoon roasted garlic
1 teaspoon fresh thyme
1 teaspoon fresh oregano
1 teaspoon fresh basil
2 cups seafood stock (may substitute chicken stock)
1 teaspoon Cajun seasoning
1 cup white wine
8 ounces Linguini or Fettuccini pasta
1 1/2 cup freshly grated Parmesan cheese
1 teaspoon unsalted butter
2 tablespoons olive oil
parsley
salt & pepper to taste

Directions

In a saucepan heat 1 tablespoon olive oil and add the celery, onion, carrots, and tomatoes. Cook until al dente. Add the roasted garlic, thyme, oregano, basil, and white wine. Allow wine to cook down halfway and then add the seafood stock. Simmer over medium heat for 20 minutes. Allow mixture to cool slightly and then place mixture in a blender or food processor and blend on low speed. Slowly add heavy cream and Parmesan cheese. Once blended return to saucepan and set aside.

In another large saucepan, boil water and add the pasta. Cook until tender and remove from heat.

In a separate sauté pan, heat 1 tablespoon of olive oil and sauté the shrimp. Sprinkle with Cajun seasoning and cook until pinkish in color. Carefully spoon the vegetable cream mixture into the sauté pan with the shrimp and add one teaspoon of butter, stirring slowing until melted. Remove shrimp mixture from heat and mix well.

Plate pasta and top with shrimp mixture. Neatly arrange shrimp and garnish with Parmesan cheese and parsley.

JAMBALAYA

Number of Servings: 8
Preparation Time: 20-30 minutes

Ingredients

3/4 cup chopped onion
1/2 cup chopped celery
1/4 cup chopped green pepper
2 garlic cloves, minced
2 tablespoons butter or margarine
2 cups diced sausage
1 (28 oz.) can diced tomatoes, undrained
1 (10 1/2 oz.) can beef broth
1 cup uncooked rice
1 cup water
1 teaspoon sugar
1 teaspoon dried thyme
1/2 teaspoon chili powder
1/4 teaspoon pepper
1 1/2 pounds fresh or frozen uncooked shrimp, peeled and deveined
1 tablespoon chopped parsley

Directions

In Dutch oven, sauté onion, celery, green pepper, and garlic in butter until tender. Add next nine ingredients, bring to a boil. Reduce heat, cover and simmer until rice is tender, about 25 minutes. Add shrimp and parsley. Simmer until shrimp is tender, approximately 7-10 minutes.

SEAFOOD CASSEROLE

Number of Servings: 6-8
Preparation Time: 45 minutes

Ingredients

1 stick margarine
1 1/2 cups chopped onions
1 1/2 cups chopped celery
1 1/2 cups chopped green onions (shallots)
1 large bell pepper
1 bag crawfish tails
1/2 pound crabmeat
2 pounds peeled shrimp
1 pound Velveeta cheese
1 cup half and half
1 1/2 pounds angel hair pasta
1/4 cup milk
1 tablespoon flour

Directions

Sauté seasoning with margarine. Add flour and seafood, cook a little while and set aside. Boil pasta separately and set aside.

Preheat oven to 350°. Begin sauce. Add a little margarine, milk, and Velveeta cheese to saucepan. Cook over low heat until cheese is melted. Stir pasta into seafood mixture. Stir in cheese sauce and spoon into casserole dish. Bake for about 10-15 minutes.

"*Huddle* with your family around the dinner table and share your daily challenges, victories, and testimonies. You will reap the benefits of a 'winning team.'"

—Bishop T.D. Jakes

SEA BASS WITH CURRY AND GINGER

Number of Servings: 6
Preparation Time: 50 minutes

Ingredients

2 cups nonfat milk
3 tablespoons minced peeled fresh ginger
1 tablespoon Thai red curry base
1 teaspoon turmeric
2 teaspoons finely chopped garlic
2 teaspoons fish sauce (nam pla)
1 1/2 teaspoons imitation coconut extract
6 (5 to 6 oz.) sea bass fillets
1/2 cup bottled clam juice
1 tablespoon arrowroot
3 tablespoons chopped fresh basil
1 tablespoon sugar
3 cups cooked jasmine rice or other white rice

Directions

Combine first 7 ingredients in glass baking dish. Add fish. Refrigerate 2 hours, turning occasionally.

Remove fish from the curry mixture. Transfer curry mixture to a heavy large skillet and bring to simmer over high heat. Sprinkle fish with salt and pepper; add fish to skillet. Reduce heat to low; cover and simmer 4 minutes. Turn fish, cover and simmer until opaque in center, about 2 minutes longer. Using spatula, transfer fish to plate. Tent with foil to keep warm.

Whisk clam juice and arrowroot in small bowl to dissolve arrowroot. Whisk into curry mixture. Boil until slightly thickened, whisking often, about 6 minutes. Stir in basil and sugar. Season with salt. Pour any accumulated juices from fish into curry sauce. Serve fish over rice and spoon sauce over fish.

PAN BROILED FISH

Number of Servings: 2
Preparation Time: 25 minutes

Ingredients

2 medium whole catfish or
4 large catfish filets
1 medium onion, chopped
1 large potatos, cubed
3/4 - 1 cup water
1/2 teaspoon salt (optional)
1 teaspoon black pepper and/or
1 tablespoon Soul Food seasoning

Directions

Wash fish. Pat dry with paper towels. Preheat large skillet until very hot. Place fish into hot skillet, skin side down. Be sure pieces are not touching each other. Immediately after placing all fish in skillet, turn filets over with a spatula. Add cut vegetables and seasonings on top of fish. Add enough water to just cover, and bring to a simmer. Cover and reduce heat. Do not stir. Cook until vegetables are done (about 5-10 minutes). With a spatula, remove fish and vegetables from skillet and place onto serving plates. Serve while hot.

Note: If deboning whole fish, the unused center-boned section can be cooked along with the filets as usual. Discard bones before serving.

SEAFOOD

STUFFED HERB CREAMED FILET MIGNON

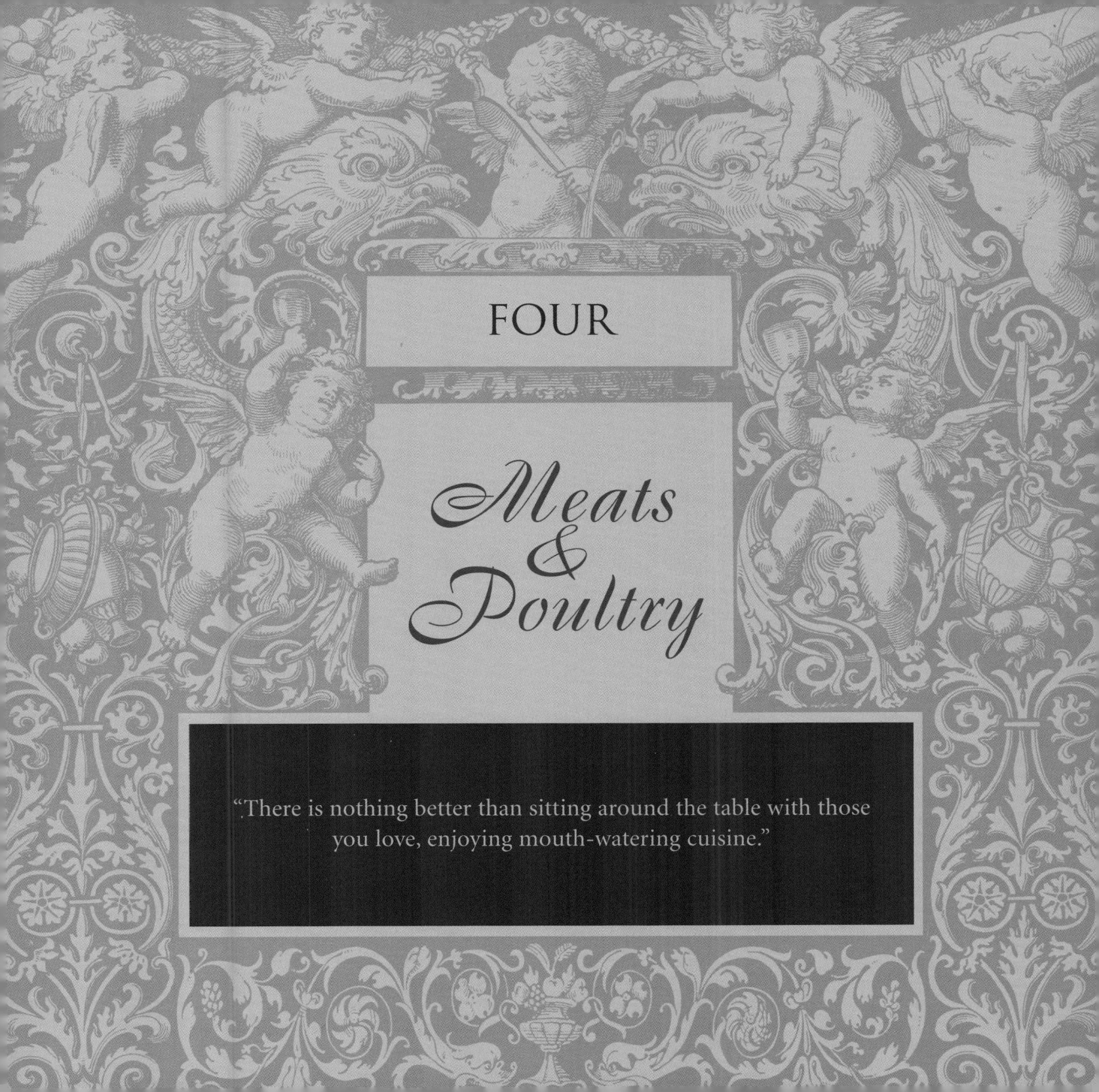

FOUR

Meats & Poultry

"There is nothing better than sitting around the table with those you love, enjoying mouth-watering cuisine."

ST. JULIEN CREOLE WING FLING

Number of Servings: 16
Preparation Time: 1 hour, 30 minutes

Ingredients

red pepper
black pepper
garlic salt
Old Bay Seasoning
1 large onion, diced
1 large bell pepper, diced
8 green onions, diced
8 garlic cloves, minced
1 cup olive oil
3 tablespoons butter
2 pounds buffalo wings
2 pounds medium shrimp, cleaned and deveined
2 pounds artificial crabmeat
1 - 2 pounds smoked sausage, thinly sliced
2 pounds cut okra
1 (8 oz.) can tomato paste
1 (12 oz.) can tomato sauce
2 cans stewed tomatoes
1 - 3 pounds rice

Directions

Bake buffalo wings according to package directions and set aside.

In a large pot, sauté onions, bell pepper, garlic, and green onion in 1/2 cup olive oil. Add okra and cook for 15 minutes, stirring frequently. Add smoked sausage, tomato sauce mixed with 1/2 cup water, tomatoes, black pepper, red pepper, and garlic salt (season to taste). Cook 15 minutes. Add tomato paste and continue to stir frequently for an additional 10 minutes. Add wings to mixture and cook for 10 minutes.

Preheat oven to 350°. While wings are cooking in mixture, mix 1/2 cup olive oil with 3 tablespoons butter, and baste crabmeat. Sprinkle crabmeat with Old Bay Seasoning and bake for 5 minutes.

Add shrimp to wing mixture, and cook for 3-5 minutes. Turn heat off. Place crabmeat around large platter of steamed rice. Serve St. Julien's Creole Wing Fling over rice. Garnish with green onion tops and fresh parsley.

CROWN ROAST TIMOTHY

Number of Servings: 6-8
Preparation Time: 2 hours

Ingredients

1 (12-14 rib) crown roast of pork
1 cup onion, chopped
1 tablespoon margarine
2 teaspoons salt
1 teaspoon dried thyme
1/2 cup orange juice
2 cups hot cooked white rice
2 cups hot cooked wild rice
1/2 cup oven roasted pecans
2 cups sweet Italian sausage
Optional: seedless grapes, star fruit, and orange

Directions

Preheat oven to 325°. Season the inside and outside of the roast with salt and pepper. Place rib side down in shallow pan and bake for 1 1/2 hours.

Meanwhile, sauté Italian sausage until done. Add onion, thyme, salt, pepper, and pecans. After 5 minutes add the orange juice. Cover and cook over low heat for about 3 minutes. Stir in cooked white and wild rice along with the orange peels. Stir to mix well.

About 15 minutes before meat is done baking, remove from oven. Pour off pan juices and reserve to make gravy. Turn rib ends up and fill center with Italian sausage and rice mixture. Cover with foil to prevent rice from drying. Return to oven until fully cooked. Remove from oven and serve on platter.

If desired, use seedless grapes, star fruit, and orange slices as a garnish.

MEATS AND POULTRY

MARINATED BEEF

Number of Servings: 8
Preparation Time: 30 minutes

Ingredients

2 pounds cooked deli roast beef (thinly sliced, not shaved), chopped
1 cup green onions, chopped
1 (8 oz.) bottle Italian dressing
1 package cherry tomatoes, sliced
3/4 head of lettuce

Directions

Combine beef, green onions, and Italian dressing. Cover and marinade 8-12 hours in refrigerator. Wash lettuce and tear into bite size pieces. Wrap lettuce in paper towels and refrigerated overnight

Before serving, drain dressing from marinated mixture. Mix sliced tomatoes in with chopped beef. Serve on a bed of lettuce with assorted crackers.

GRILLED INDIAN-STYLE CHICKEN WITH YOGURT SAUCE

Number of Servings: 4-6
Preparation Time: 1 hour

Ingredients

2 cups plain yogurt
2 teaspoons cumin seeds
2 carrots
1/4 cup finely chopped fresh mint leaves
3 pounds chicken wings (12 to 14)
1 cup coarse salt
2 cups water
1 1/2 tablespoons garam masala (Indian spice mix)
1 tablespoon vegetable oil

Directions

To make the sauce, drain yogurt in a sieve set over a bowl. Cover and chill for 2 hours. In a dry small heavy skillet, toast cumin seeds over moderate heat for about 2 to 3 minutes, shaking the skillet frequently, until seeds are a shade darker. Cool cumin seeds and coarsely grind with a mortar and pestle or in an electric coffee or spice grinder. Finely grate carrots into a bowl and stir in yogurt, cumin, mint, and salt and pepper to taste. Sauce may be made up to 8 hours ahead and chilled.

Cut off wing tips, reserving for another use, and halve wings at the joint. In a large bowl dissolve coarse salt in water. Place wings in the brine, cover, and chill in the refrigerator. Marinate for at least 2 hours and up to 24 hours, stirring occasionally.

Prepare grill.

In a colander drain wings and rinse well. Pat wings dry and in a separate bowl rub garam masala and oil onto wings. Grill wings on an oiled rack set 5 to 6 inches over glowing coals until cooked through and golden brown, about 8 to 10 minutes on each side.

Serve wings with sauce.

MEATS AND POULTRY

CROWN ROAST TIMOTHY

"*Honor* your family—prepare each meal as though you are serving kings and queens."

—Bishop T.D. Jakes

BAKED CHICKEN WINGS

Number of Servings: 4-6
Preparation Time: 25 minutes

Ingredients

1 package chicken wings
1/2 cup vinegar
1/2 cup soy sauce
1 cup water
white or black ground pepper

DIRECTIONS

Mix vinegar, soy sauce, and water. Add wings to mixture and marinate approximately 6-8 hours or overnight.

Remove wings from marinade and sprinkle pepper over wings to lightly coat. Place in a baking dish and cover. Bake in 375°-400° oven for approximately 1 hour. Remove and enjoy with steamed rice or vegetables

JOAN'S BARBECUE RIBS

Number of Servings: 6
Preparation Time: 30 minutes

Ingredients

2 slabs baby back ribs
Worcestershire sauce
rib seasoning
seasoned meat tenderizer
barbecue sauce

DIRECTIONS

Season ribs with tenderizer and rib seasoning. Cover and refrigerate overnight.

The following day, remove ribs from refrigerator and pour Worcestershire sauce over them. Let ribs marinate while preparing your grill.

Grill over hot coals using standing sauce (Worcestershire) to coat while grilling

15 minutes before ribs are done coat with your favorite barbecue sauce then remove from grill and enjoy.

MEATS AND POULTRY

CROCK POT STEW

Number of Servings: 4
Preparation Time: 8 hours

Ingredients

1 pound lean ground beef
1 pound chili grind beef meat
1 can golden mushroom soup
1 can creamy chicken mushroom soup
1 can cream of mushroom soup
1 (16 oz.) package frozen green beans
1 (16 oz.) package frozen stew vegetables
1 package Lipton's Beefy Onion Soup Mix

DIRECTIONS

Combine all ingredients in the crock-pot and cook on high for 6-8 hours. Do not add water to the mix. This makes a delicious, rich bean stew. It is easy to prepare and can be left unattended while it cooks.

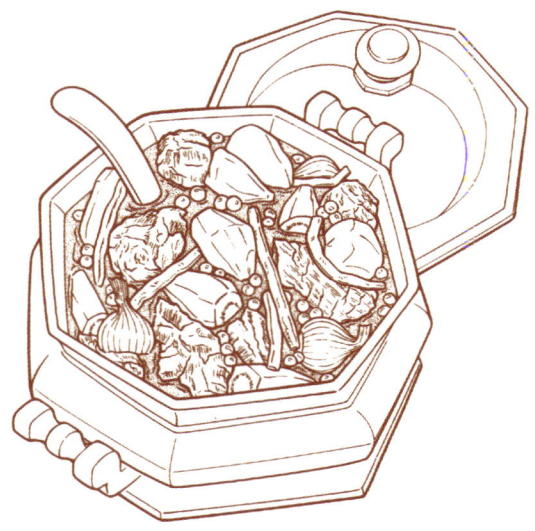

ADOBE CHICKEN

Number of Servings: 8
Preparation Time: 2 hours

Ingredients

whole chicken, cut up in serving pieces
2 whole lemons
1/4 cup cumin
1/4 cup thyme
1/4 cup black pepper
4 basil leaves, dried
4 cups cooked white rice
1 cup vinegar

Directions

Clean chicken well. Boil in large pot with all seasonings until meat starts to pull away from bones. Let water come to a rapid boil then let simmer. During cooking time season more to taste and add salt if desired.

Cook rice according to package directions. Serve chicken over rice and squeeze fresh lemon juice on top.

Suggested side dish: Chilled cucumbers, tomatoes, and red onions marinated in vinegar overnight.

CURRIED GOAT

Number of Servings: 6-8
Preparation Time: 45 minutes

Ingredients

3 pounds chopped goat meat
1 red bell pepper, chopped
1 green bell pepper, chopped
1 tablespoon curry powder
2 bulbs garlic
1 onion, chopped
1/4 cup parsley, chopped
1 bunch chives, chopped
1/4 cup celery
1 tablespoon Creole seasoning
1 teaspoon oil
1 teaspoon garlic, minced
1 teaspoon black pepper
1 teaspoon sugar

Directions

Combine bell peppers, curry powder, garlic, onion, parsley, chives, celery, and Creole seasoning in a large bowl. Marinate chopped goat meat in the mixture for about 20-30 minutes.

In a large pot or pressure cooker add oil, garlic, ground black pepper, and 1 teaspoon granulated sugar. Bring to a boil until brown. Add marinated meat to pot. Slow cook marinated meat until tender. Serve over rice.

SPICY TURKEY AND RICE

Number of Servings: 4
Preparation Time: 1 hour, 35 minutes

Ingredients

2 cups chicken broth
1 teaspoon basil
1/4 teaspoon garlic powder
1/4 teaspoon hot pepper sauce
1 (14.5 oz.) can freshly stewed tomatoes
2 cups long-grain white rice, cooked
1 cup frozen green peas, thawed
2 cups light turkey meat, skinless, cooked, and cubed

Directions

Mix broth, basil, garlic powder, hot pepper sauce, and tomatoes in a medium saucepan. Over medium-high heat, bring to a boil. Stir in rice and reduce heat to low. Cover and cook 20 minutes. Stir in peas and turkey. Cover and cook 5 minutes or until rice is done.

Optional: For reduced sodium and fat, substitute fat free, low sodium chicken broth and low sodium or sodium free canned tomatoes.

MEATS AND POULTRY

STUFFED CHICKEN

Number of Servings: 2-4
Preparation Time: 45 minutes

Ingredients

2 (6 oz.) chicken breasts
1 cup of fresh cooked spinach
1 cup Italian mushrooms, chopped
1/2 cup fresh mozzarella cheese
2 tablespoons fresh basil, sliced julienne
8 ounces organic sun dried tomato pasta
3 tablespoons olive oil
1 tablespoon salt
1 tablespoon roasted garlic
1 Roma tomato
1 tablespoon fresh sun dried tomatoes
juice of one whole lemon
cooking twine or rope (for binding chicken breast)
salt & pepper to taste

Directions

Preheat oven to 350°. In a small bowl, combine spinach, mushrooms, basil, and mozzarella cheese. Set aside.

Tenderize the chicken breasts by pounding flat to 1/2 inch thickness. Season both sides of chicken with salt and pepper. Fill each chicken breast with equal amounts of the spinach mixture, being careful not to overstuff. Roll each chicken breast closed and tie with cooking twine.

Heat 1 tablespoon of olive oil in an ovenproof sauté pan. Add chicken breast to pan and brown on all sides. Place pan in preheated oven for approximately 10 minutes.

Meanwhile, boil water for the pasta. Once water is boiling, add salt and the pasta, being careful not to overcook. In a separate sauté pan heat 1 tablespoon of olive oil and the roasted garlic. Once warm, add sun dried tomatoes and lemon juice. Sauté until tender and then remove from heat.

Toss pasta in sauté mixture and plate. Remove chicken breast from oven and remove cooking twine. Slice each piece of chicken into circular slices and place on top of plated pasta. Garnish with diced Roma tomatoes and fresh basil.

STUFFED CHICKEN

FIVE

Breads

"The strength of the family is greatest when we all work together toward the same goals."

MAMA'S SWEET POTATO BREAD

Number of Servings: 10-12
Preparation Time: 20 minutes

Ingredients

2 large cans sweet potatoes, drained
2 cups flour
1 cup white corn meal
2 1/2 cups sugar
1/2 pound butter, melted
pinch of salt
2 teaspoons baking powder
1 teaspoon pure vanilla extract
1 teaspoon lemon flavoring
6 eggs
1 can evaporated milk (regular size)
nutmeg to taste

Directions

Preheat oven to 450°. Combine all ingredients together in a large bowl. Mix well until batter achieves a smooth texture.

Pour batter into prepared loaf pans and bake for 15 minutes. Reduce oven temperature to 350°, and bake for an additional 45 minutes.

SPICY MATZO BREI

Number of Servings: 4-6
Preparation Time: 20-30 minutes

Ingredients

1 1/2 squares Matzo
1 tablespoon unsalted butter
3/4 cup chopped onion
3/4 cup chopped celery
1/2 fresh jalapeno pepper, minced
pinch of sugar
1 medium clove garlic, minced
1 large egg or
3 tablespoons egg substitute
1 tablespoon water
1/8 teaspoon salt
ground pepper

Directions

In a medium bowl, break the matzo into pieces about 1 inch in size. Cover the matzo with warm water and allow it to sit for a few minutes until soft. Drain the water, gently pressing out any excess from the matzo.

In a medium skillet over medium heat, melt butter. Add the onions, celery, and jalapeno pepper, sprinkle with a pinch of sugar and sauté, stirring occasionally, until the onions begin to brown. Add the garlic and sauté for 1 minute or until it softens. Add the matzo and fry for about 3 minutes to dry it slightly.

Meanwhile, in a medium bowl, beat the egg with the water, salt, and pepper.

To use as a stuffing, spoon the matzo mixture into the egg mixture and stir until incorporated.

BROCCOLI CORNBREAD

Number of Servings: 10
Preparation Time: 10 minutes

Ingredients

2 boxes Jiffy Cornbread Mix
4 eggs
1 finely grated onion
8 oz. sour cream
2 sticks melted butter
1 package frozen chopped broccoli
(drain well)

Directions

Combine all ingredients and mix well. Bake at $350°$ for 45 minutes

BUTTERMILK BISCUITS

Number of Servings: 6
Preparation Time: 25 minutes

Ingredients

1 3/4 cups flour
1 teaspoon salt
3 teaspoons baking powder
1 teaspoon sugar
1/2 teaspoon baking soda
4 tablespoons lard
2/3 cup buttermilk

Directions

Sift flour, baking powder, salt, and baking soda into a large bowl. Add sugar and cut lard into flour. Add the buttermilk and stir until mixture forms a ball. Roll dough out about 1/4" thick on a clean white dishcloth that has been floured. Cut dough with a cookie cutter. Place biscuits in a well-greased pan. Bake in a 400° oven until golden brown.

BANANA NUT BREAD

Number of Servings: 24
Preparation Time: 45 minutes

Ingredients

1 1/4 cups sugar
1/2 cup (1 stick) margarine or butter (softened)
2 eggs
1 1/2 cups mashed ripe bananas (about 3 medium)
1/2 cup buttermilk
1 teaspoon vanilla
2 1/2 cups all-purpose flour
2 teaspoons baking powder
1/2 teaspoon salt
1/4 teaspoon baking soda
1 cup chopped walnuts or pecans

Directions

Pre-heat oven to 350°. Grease bottoms only of two 8 1/2" loaf pans, or one 9" loaf pan. Mix sugar and margarine in a large bowl. Stir in eggs. Add bananas, buttermilk, and vanilla, beat until smooth. Stir in flour, baking powder, salt, and baking soda just until flour is moistened. Stir in walnuts. Pour into prepared loaf pans.

Bake 8-inch loaves for approximately 1 hour; 9-inch loaf for 1 hour 15 minutes or until toothpick inserted in center comes out clean. Cool 5 minutes. Loosen sides of loaves from pans; remove from pans. Cool completely on wire rack before slicing. Store tightly wrapped in refrigerator for up to 1 week.

MEATY CORNBREAD

Number of Servings: 10 to 12
Preparation Time: 1 hour, 15 minutes

Ingredients

1 pound chicken livers or gizzards
2 pounds turkey necks
1 1/2 packages sage sausage
2 cups chopped celery
2 cups chopped onions
2 cups chopped green peppers
(For personal preference, may add more or less celery, onions, and peppers.)
1/2 stick margarine
4 large eggs
4 boxes Jiffy mix
3 1/4 cups milk
2 cans beef or chicken broth

Directions

Broil chicken livers or gizzards and turkey necks in large pan (season to taste). Fry sage sausage in large skillet. After meats have finished cooking, let cool for 10 minutes, then chop meats to your satisfaction. Prepare Jiffy mix as recommended. Sauté chopped celery, onions, and green peppers in a small pan for 3 minutes, then add broth.

Preheat oven to 350°. Blend all the ingredients together in a large bowl, and slowly add broth to mixture. Once all the ingredients have been successfully combined, place in large cake pan (12" x 9") and bake for 15-20 minutes or until golden brown.

PECAN PIE SUPREME

SIX

Desserts

"Your family is the most important enterprise in which you can ever invest."

NEIMAN MARCUS CAKE

Number of Servings: 10-12
Preparation Time: 25 minutes

Ingredients

1 box yellow cake mix
1/2 cup melted butter
1 egg
1 (8 oz.) package cream cheese
2 eggs
1 pound powered sugar

Directions

Preheat oven to 350°. Grease a 9" x 13" cake pan. Mix first three ingredients until moist. Press into bottom of pan. Mix next 3 ingredients and pour on top of first layer. Bake for 30-40 minutes (will be gooey in center).

GLENN'S FAVORITE CHOCOLATE SHEET CAKE

Number of Servings: 10-12
Preparation Time: 45 minutes

Ingredients

2 cups sugar
2 cups flour
1 teaspoon cinnamon
1 teaspoon baking soda
1/2 cup of Crisco
1 stick of butter
1 cup of water
4 tablespoons cocoa
1 teaspoon vanilla
2 eggs, slightly beaten
1/2 cup buttermilk

DIRECTIONS

Preheat oven to 350°. In a large bowl, combine sugar, flour, cinnamon, and baking soda. Mix well and set aside. In a saucepan add the Crisco, butter, water, and cocoa. Bring to a boil and pour over the flour and sugar mixture. Then add the vanilla, eggs, and buttermilk, and mix well.

Pour into well-greased 10 1/4" x 13" pan and bake for 30 minutes, until mixture pulls away from sides of pan and springs back when lightly touched in the center.

ICING

Ingredients

4 tablespoons cocoa
6 tablespoons milk
1 stick butter (softened)
1 box powered sugar
2 teaspoons vanilla extract
1 cup pecan pieces

DIRECTIONS

While cake is baking (about 5 minutes before it is done), mix all six ingredients.

Pour the mixture over hot cake and serve.

CREAM CHEESE FLAN

Number of Servings: 8
Preparation Time: 1 hour

Ingredients

1 cup sugar
1/2 cup water
1 1/2 cups evaporated milk
1 1/4 cups sweetened condensed milk
1 (8 oz.) package cream cheese, softened
1/2 cup butter, softened
5 eggs
1 teaspoon pure vanilla extract
8 (8 oz.) custard cups

Directions

Preheat oven to 350° and prepare large pan or pans for water bath. In a medium saucepan, mix the sugar and water together and cook over low heat. Stir the mixture constantly for 3 to 4 minutes or until dissolved. Then increase heat to medium-high and boil without stirring, for about 15 minutes or until caramel colored. Quickly pour over bottom and sides of the custard cups (if mixture begins to harden, soften over low heat).

Combine evaporated milk, sweetened condensed milk, cream cheese, butter, eggs, and vanilla in a blender, food processor, or electric mixer bowl. Blend well. Pour mixture into prepared custard cups. Arrange custard cups in one or two pans prepared for water bath, and pour in hot water to a depth of 1 inch. Bake for 35 to 45 minutes or until knife inserted near center comes out clean. Cool on wire racks for 20 minutes, then chill for several hours. Run knife around rims gently and invert onto serving plates.

STRAWBERRY DREAM CAKE

STRAWBERRY DREAM CAKE

Number of Servings: 8-10
Preparation Time: 1 hour, 45 minutes

Ingredients

3/4 cup butter
2 cups sugar
3 cups sifted cake flour
1 tablespoon baking power
1/2 teaspoon salt
1 cup milk
1 teaspoon pure vanilla extract
5 egg whites
1 (3 oz.) package strawberry gelatin
1 pint fresh strawberries (save four for top of cake)
Cream Cheese Frosting
Strawberry Glaze

Directions

Preheat oven to 375°. Prepare 3 nine inch round cake pans, butter and flour each, then set aside.

Cream butter, sugar, and vanilla until light and fluffy. Sift cake flour with baking power, gelatin, and salt, and add to cream mixture alternating with the milk. Beat well. Chop strawberries and add to mixture and stir. In a separate bowl beat egg whites until stiff peaks form. Fold whites into the batter until no streaks remain.

Divide batter into prepared cake pans. Reduce heat in oven to 350° and bake for 25 minutes or until a wooden pick is inserted and comes out clean. Cool cake on wire racks.

When cool apply Cream Cheese Frosting, Strawberry Glaze, and top with remaining strawberries.

CREAM CHEESE FROSTING

Ingredients

3 tablespoons butter
4 cups confectioners sugar
1 teaspoon pure vanilla extract
2 (8 oz.) packages cream cheese

Directions

Cream the cream cheese and butter together, then gradually add the confectioners sugar until light and fluffy. Mix in the pure vanilla extract until well incorporated. Spread between layers, on top and sides of cooled cake.

STRAWBERRY GLAZE

Ingredients

1 1/2 pints fresh strawberries
1 package strawberry gelatin
1/2 cup sugar
1 tablespoon lemon juice
1 tablespoon red food coloring
2 teaspoons Marsala

Directions

Puree strawberries and pour into a medium bowl. Prepare gelatin according to package directions (do not chill) and pour directly into the pureed strawberries. Stir in the remaining ingredients and blend well until mixture is smooth and can be spread easily. Spoon glaze on top of frosted cake, allowing it to run down the sides.

SINGLE CRUST PASTRY

Ingredients

1 1/4 cups all-purpose flour
1/4 teaspoon salt
1/3 cup vegetable shortening
4 to 5 tablespoons cold water

Directions

Sift the flour and salt together. Cut in the shortening until the pieces are the size of small peas. Sprinkle one tablespoon of water over part of the mixture: gently toss with a fork. Push to the side of the bowl. Repeat the process until all of the mixture is moistened and forms a ball. Lightly flour surface and roll dough to a 12-inch circle. Line the pie pan with the rolled dough and trim to 1/2 inch beyond edge. Fold under extra pastry and flute edges.

PECAN PIE SUPREME

Number of Servings: 6-8
Preparation Time: 1 hour

Ingredients

Single Crust Pie Pastry
3 slightly beaten eggs
1 cup light corn syrup
3/4 cup sugar
3 tablespoons brown sugar
3 tablespoons butter, softened
1 teaspoon pure vanilla extract
1/8 teaspoon salt
1/2 cup chopped pecans
1 1/2 cups pecan halves

Directions

Prepare crust for a 9-inch pie pan using pastry recipe on previous page. Do not prick or precook. Set aside until filling has been prepared.

Preheat oven to 350°. In a large mixing bowl combine eggs, corn syrup, sugar, brown sugar, butter, vanilla, and salt. Mix well. Stir in the chopped pecans. Pour filling into prepared pie crust and arrange pecan halves on top.

Bake for 30 minutes, then cover the edges of the crust with foil to prevent over-browning and bake for an additional 25-30 minutes. To test for doneness, insert a knife near the center. If it comes out clean, the pie is done.

Place pie on wire rack and cool.

CREAM CHEESE POUND CAKE

Number of Servings: 12-15
Preparation Time: 45 minutes

Ingredients

3 sticks butter
3 cups flour
1 (8 oz.) package cream cheese
3 cups sugar
6 eggs
1 teaspoon pure vanilla extract

Directions

Preheat oven to 325°. Beat cream cheese and butter together until it looks like vanilla ice cream. Add sugar gradually. Alternate adding flour and eggs. Add vanilla and mix well. Pour batter into greased cake pans and bake for 1 hour and 20 minutes.

CARAMEL FROSTING

Ingredients

3/4 cup butter or margarine
1 1/2 cups packed brown sugar
6 tablespoons carnation milk
2 1/2 cups sifted powdered sugar

Directions

Place butter and brown sugar in saucepan. Heat and stir to boiling. Boil for 2 minutes, stirring constantly. Stir in evaporated milk, cool until warm to touch.

Stir in powdered sugar, 1/2 cup at a time. If frosting is too thin, add more powdered sugar. Spread over cake.

GERMAN CHOCOLATE CAKE

Number of Servings: 10-12
Preparation Time: 1 hour

Ingredients

1/2 cup water
6 oz. Baker's Sweet German Chocolate, chopped
2 1/4 cups all purpose flour
1 1/2 teaspoons baking soda
1/4 teaspoon salt
2 cups sugar
1 cup (2 sticks) unsalted butter, room temperature
4 large eggs, separated
2 teaspoons pure vanilla extract
1 cup buttermilk

Directions

Preheat oven to 350°. Butter a 13 x 9 inch glass baking dish and set aside. Bring water to simmer in small saucepan. Reduce heat to low. Add chopped chocolate; whisk until smooth. Cool.

Sift flour, baking soda, and salt into a medium bowl. Using electric mixer, beat sugar and butter in large bowl until well blended. Beat in yolks, 1 at a time. Mix in chocolate mixture and vanilla.

Add dry ingredients to batter, alternating with buttermilk. Using clean dry beaters, beat egg whites in another large bowl until stiff but not dry. Fold into batter in two additions. Pour batter into prepared dish. Bake until tester inserted in center comes out clean, about 1 hour. Cool cake in pan on rack.

FROSTING

Ingredients

1 (12 oz.) can evaporated milk
1 1/2 cups sugar
3/4 cup (1 1/2 sticks) unsalted butter
5 large egg yolks
1/4 teaspoon almond extract
1 (7 oz.) package sweetened, shredded coconut
1 1/2 cups coarsely chopped pecans

Directions

Combine first 5 ingredients in a large, heavy saucepan. Whisk over medium-high heat until mixture simmers, thickens, and leaves path on back of spoon when finger is drawn across, about 18 minutes. Mix in coconut and pecans. Spread warm frosting over cake.

DESSERTS

PEANUT BUTTER THUMBPRINTS

Number of Servings: About 3 dozen cookies
Preparation Time: 1 hour

Ingredients

1 cup butter
2 cups light brown sugar
1 1/2 cups peanut butter
2 eggs
1 teaspoon vanilla
2 1/2 cups flour
1 teaspoon baking powder
1 teaspoon baking soda
1 3/4 cups unsalted dry roasted peanuts, finely chopped

Directions

Cream butter, brown sugar, and peanut butter together. Add the eggs and vanilla. Sift dry ingredients together in a separate bowl and add to creamed mixture, mixing well.

Shape dough into 1" balls. Roll balls in the finely chopped peanuts. Place on baking sheet. Place a thumbprint indentation on each before baking. Bake at 350° for approximately 10-12 minutes.

CHOCOLATE FILLING

Ingredients

3 oz. cream cheese
3 tablespoons light corn syrup
1/2 teaspoon pure vanilla extract
1 cup chocolate chips, melted
1/2 cup powdered sugar

Directions

Melt chocolate and cool to room temperature. Cream the cream cheese and add the chocolate, corn syrup, vanilla, and powdered sugar, mixing well. Place a small spoonful of filling in each cookie.

BANANA PUDDING

Number of Servings: 8-10
Preparation Time: 45 minutes

Ingredients

1 box Nabisco Vanilla Wafers
4-6 ripe bananas
1 can Eagle Brand Condensed Milk
1 box Jello French Vanilla Pudding Mix
1 1/2 cups water
small container of heavy whipping cream
pecans or walnuts, optional

Directions

In large bowl combine the condensed milk, pudding mix, and water, and mix well at high speed. Place in refrigerator.

In a separate bowl, blend whipping cream at high speed until it doubles in content. Remove the pudding from the refrigerator and fold in the whipped cream.

Prepare a third bowl with a layer of crumbled wafers, and top with sliced bananas. Pour pudding over cookies and bananas. Crumble wafers to coat top of pudding, then line bowl with whole wafers. Add pecans or walnuts, if desired. Refrigerate until molded.

> "*Cooking* can be the perfect illustration of "family": a group of people working together for the good of the whole."
> —Bishop T.D. Jakes

DESSERTS

EGG PIE

Number of Servings: 8
Preparation Time: 35 minutes

Ingredients

1 cup sugar
3 eggs
1 cup milk
1 tablespoon butter
1/4 teaspoon nutmeg
1 teaspoon pure vanilla extract

Directions

Preheat oven to 400°. In large bowl, beat eggs and sugar together. Boil milk until thoroughly heated. Add butter to hot milk. Combine milk mixture with sugar and egg mixture. Beat in vanilla. Pour mixture into an unbaked, shallow pie crust. Sprinkle nutmeg on top of pie. Bake for 15 minutes. Then reduce oven temperature to 350° and bake an additional 25 minutes. Serve warm or chilled.

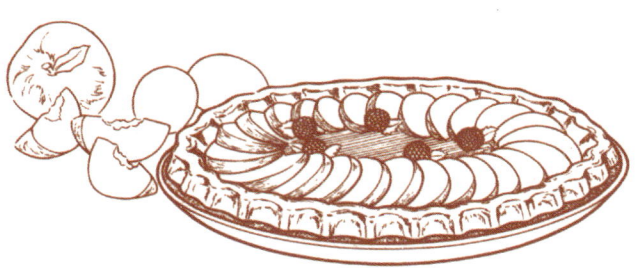

AUNT LEANNA'S POUND CAKE

Number of Servings: 8
Preparation Time: 50 minutes

Ingredients

1 (8 oz.) package cream cheese
3 sticks butter
3 cups sugar
6 eggs
1 1/2 teaspoons orange flavoring
1 1/2 teaspoons lemon flavoring
3 cups of Swans Down Cake Flour

Directions

Preheat oven to 325°. Cream the butter, sugar, and cream cheese. Add the eggs, one at a time, and both flavorings, mixing well. Slowly add flour to the batter and mix well. Pour batter into greased pan, and bake in center of oven for 1 hour and 25 minutes. Let cool for 25 minutes before removing from pan.

ICING

Ingredients

1 1/2 tablespoons of lemon juice (1/2 squeezed lemon)
1/2 cup powdered sugar

Directions

Mix lemon juice and powdered sugar and pour over top of cake. The cake can be completely cooled, however, it will soak up the icing better if it is warm.

DESSERTS

CHOCOLATE DELIGHT

Number of Servings: 12 to 16
Preparation Time: 2 days

Ingredients

1 cup chopped pecans
1 cup flour
1 stick butter or margarine
1 (8 oz.) package cream cheese, room temperature
1 cup cool whip, room temperature
1 cup powdered sugar
1 package instant chocolate pudding mix
1 package instant vanilla pudding mix
1 teaspoon pure vanilla extract
3 cups milk

Directions

Preheat oven to 350°. Mix pecans, flour, and butter together and press into the bottom of a 9 x 13 inch pan. Bake for 20 minutes. Set pan aside and let cool.

Combine cream cheese, cool whip, and powdered sugar. Mix well and spread on top of cooled crust to form second layer. Chill overnight

The next day, combine the chocolate pudding mix, vanilla pudding mix, vanilla extract, and milk. Blend well and spread on top of previous layer. Spread remaining cool whip on top and chill.

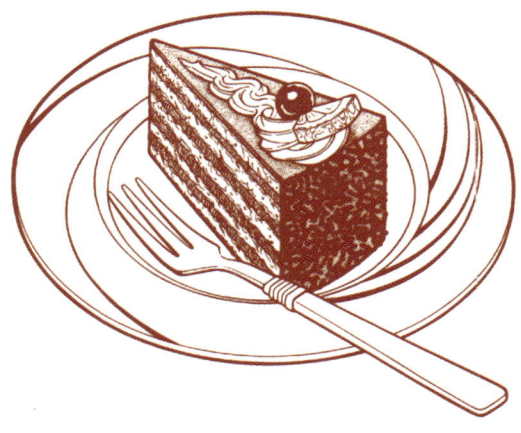

FLAN DE QUESO (CREAM CHEESE CUSTARD)

Number of Servings: 10-12
Preparation Time: 45 minutes

Ingredients

1 cup sugar
2 tablespoons water
1 (16 oz.) can condensed milk
1 (16 oz.) can evaporated milk
1 (16 oz.) can regular milk
5 eggs
1 (8 oz.) package cream cheese
1 tablespoon pure vanilla extract

Directions

In small saucepan combine sugar and water. Cook over medium to high heat, stirring constantly until all the sugar is melted and the mixture is browned, with a caramel texture. Pour into a 3 quart microwave safe dish. Set aside to cool.

Soften the cream cheese (on the microwave defrost setting) for 2-3 minutes, and set aside. Separate the eggs and place the yolks in a large mixing bowl. (Keep the egg whites.) Combine the egg yolks, condensed milk, evaporated milk, regular milk, and vanilla.

Once all ingredients are mixed well, add the softened cream cheese to the filling and blend. Then mix the egg whites until they become foamy and add to the main mix. Blend together for about 2 minutes, then pour the entire mix into the cooled caramel dish. Cover dish and bake the flan in the microwave for 18 minutes.

Carefully remove from microwave, uncover and let it stand for 20-30 minutes. Refrigerate for at least 1 to 1 1/2 hours before serving. When ready to serve, place large plate over the flan dish and turn it upside down so the flan falls on the plate. Cut and serve.

LIL' RICH POUND CAKE

Number of Servings: 8-10
Preparation Time: 45 minutes

Ingredients

3 cups silk cake flour
3 cups sugar
3 sticks melted butter
6 eggs
1 (8 oz.) package cream cheese
1 package dream whip (Jello)
2 teaspoons lemon flavor
1 teaspoon pure vanilla extract

Directions

Preheat oven to 350°. Spray cake pan with non-fat cooking spray (or grease and flour) and set aside.

In a large mixing bowl, combine sugar, butter, and cream cheese. Blend well and add the dream whip, lemon flavoring, and vanilla. Once mixture is smooth, add the eggs, one at a time. Slowly add the silk cake flour. (Silk cake flour or swan down cake flour is recommended because it has a finer texture.) Bake for 1 hour, 15 minutes.

CHOCOLATE-HAZELNUT WAFFLES WITH VANILLA ICE CREAM AND FUDGE SAUCE

Number of Servings: 6
Preparation Time: 50 minutes

Ingredients

1 cup sugar
3/4 cup unbleached all purpose flour
3/4 cup cake flour
1/3 cup unsweetened cocoa powder (preferably Dutch-process)
1 1/2 teaspoons baking powder
1/2 teaspoon baking soda
1/4 teaspoon salt
6 tablespoons warm water
1 teaspoon instant espresso powder
2 1/2 ounces unsweetened chocolate, chopped
3 tablespoons unsalted butter
2 tablespoons vegetable oil
1 1/2 teaspoons vanilla extract
2 extra-large eggs
1 1/4 cups buttermilk
1/2 cup hazelnuts, toasted, husked, and finely ground in processor
1/4 cup Frangelico (hazelnut liqueur) or amaretto
fudge sauce
powdered sugar
vanilla ice cream
English toffee bits (such as Skor or Heath)
chopped toasted hazelnuts

Directions

Whisk first 7 ingredients in a large bowl to blend. Stir 6 tablespoons warm water and espresso powder in small bowl until powder dissolves. Stir chocolate and butter in heavy medium saucepan over low heat until melted and smooth. Remove from heat. Whisk in oil, vanilla, and espresso mixture. Cool to lukewarm.

Whisk eggs into chocolate mixture, then 1 1/4 cups buttermilk and ground hazelnuts. Add chocolate mixture to dry ingredients and whisk to blend well.

Preheat waffle iron to medium heat, following manufacturer's instructions. Pour about 1/2 to 3/4 cup batter (depending on size of waffle iron) into center of waffle iron; spread evenly with spatula. Close waffle iron and cook about 4 minutes (time will vary, depending on waffle iron) until waffle is cooked through but still soft and color on outside darkens. Using spatula, transfer waffle to rack. Repeat with remaining batter. (Can be prepared 6 hours ahead. Let waffles stand at room temperature. Before continuing, transfer to baking sheet and warm in a 400° oven until crisp, about 6 minutes.)

Warm fudge sauce and stir in liqueur. Cut each waffle diagonally in half, forming triangles. Arrange 3 waffle triangles on each of 6 plates. Dust with powdered sugar. Place scoop of ice cream atop waffle triangles. Pour fudge sauce over waffels and ice cream. Sprinkle with toffee.

DON'T LAST LONG CAKE

Number of Servings: 10-12
Preparation Time: 25 minutes

Ingredients

2 cups flour
2 cups sugar
1/4 teaspoon salt
1 teaspoon cinnamon
1 teaspoon baking soda
3 eggs
1 1/4 cups oil
1 (15 oz.) can crushed pineapple, drained
1 cup chopped pecans
1 teaspoon pure vanilla extract
1 cup sliced bananas

Directions

Preheat oven to 325°.

Mix together oil, eggs, sugar, salt, baking soda, cinnamon, and flour. Then add the remaining ingredients. Mix well. Pour into a greased and floured bundt pan. Bake for 1 1/2 hours.

SWEET POTATO PIE

Number of Servings: 8
Preparation Time: 35 minutes

Ingredients

2 large sweet potatoes, cooked and mashed
1/2 cup skim milk
1/2 cup maple syrup
1 teaspoon pure vanilla extract
1/4 teaspoon nutmeg
2 eggs

DIRECTIONS

Boil sweet potatoes until soft and mash them in a large mixing bowl. Combine mashed sweet potatoes with eggs, syrup, vanilla, milk, and nutmeg. Mix well. Spray 9-inch pie pan with non-fat cooking spray. Pour mixture into the prepared pan and bake at 350° for 1 hour or until knife comes out clean.

GRANDMA'S FAVORITE POUND CAKE

Number of Servings: 8
Preparation Time: 1 hour, 15 minutes

Ingredients

3 sticks butter (softened)
1 (8 oz.) package of cream cheese, softened
3 cups sugar
6 eggs
1 teaspoon pure vanilla extract
1 teaspoon rum flavoring
1 teaspoon orange extract
1 teaspoon lemon extract
1 teaspoon coconut extract
3 cups all purpose flour, sifted

Directions

Cream together the butter and cream cheese. Add sugar and continue to cream. Once smooth, add eggs one at a time, until well mixed. Blend in each flavor, until well mixed. Blend in flour, a little at a time, until smooth.

Bake at 325° for 1 hour, 15 minutes (or until toothpick comes out clean) on top rack in oven in a 10" fluted bundt cake pan.

MULTI-CHOCOLATE CHIP COOKIES

Number of Servings: 3-4 dozen cookies
Preparation Time: 15 minutes

Ingredients

1 cup sugar
1 cup brown sugar
1 cup butter (softened)
2 eggs
2 teaspoons pure vanilla extract
3 cups all purpose flour
1 teaspoon salt
1 teaspoon baking soda
12-16 oz. of mixed chips (semi-sweet, milk chocolate, mint chocolate, and white chocolate)
1/2 cup chopped pecans

Directions

Preheat oven to 375°.

Blend sugars, butter, eggs, and vanilla until smooth. Mix dry ingredients, then add a little at a time to creamed butter mixture. Beat on low for about 2 minutes. Add chips and nuts and fold in gently.

Drop by small ice-cream scoop or teaspoon onto greased cookie sheet about 2 inches apart. Bake for 10-12 minutes. Cool on rack.

DESSERTS

SOUTHERN POUND CAKE

Number of Servings: 16-18
Preparation Time: 15 minutes

Ingredients

3 cups sugar
1 stick margarine
1 stick butter
1/2 cup vegetable oil
5 eggs
3 1/2 cups all purpose flour (sifted)
1 teaspoon baking powder
1/2 teaspoon salt
1 cup sour cream
1 teaspoon vanilla
1 teaspoon lemon or almond flavoring

Directions

Preheat oven to 325°. Grease and flour a 10-12 inch bundt pan. Cream sugar, softened butter, margarine, and oil until smooth. Beat in eggs one at a time until blended.

Combine dry ingredients together and mix in alternately with sour cream. Blend in flavorings. Pour into pan and bake 1 hour and 20 minutes or until golden. Cool in pan for 15 minutes, turn onto plate.

HEAVENLY DELIGHT

Number of Servings: 12
Preparation Time: 7 minutes

Ingredients

2 (24 oz.) containers cottage cheese
2 cans pineapple tidbits, drain juice
1/2 cup pecan halves or pieces
1 (10 oz.) bag small marshmallows
fresh mint leaves

DIRECTIONS

Mix cottage cheese, pineapple, and marshmallows in a large mixing bowl. Add 1/2 cup pecan pieces. Pour into dish and top with pecan halves, pineapple slices, and mint leaves.

DESSERTS

SEVEN

International

"Every family is unique."

Jamaican "Jerk" Chicken Wings

Number of Servings: 4 to 6
Preparation Time: 30 minutes

Ingredients

1 onion, chopped
2/3 cup finely chopped scallions
2 garlic cloves
1/2 teaspoon dried thyme, crumbled
1 1/2 teaspoons salt
1 1/2 teaspoons ground allspice
1/4 teaspoon freshly grated nutmeg
1/2 teaspoon cinnamon
1 teaspoon black pepper
6 drops of Tabasco, or to taste
2 tablespoons soy sauce
1/4 cup vegetable oil
18 chicken wings (about 3 1/4 pounds), with tips removed

Directions

To make the marinade, puree the onion, scallions, garlic, thyme, salt, allspice, nutmeg, cinnamon, black pepper, Tabasco, soy sauce, and oil in a food processor or blender.

In a large shallow baking dish arrange the wings in a single layer and spoon the marinade over them, rubbing in well (wear rubber gloves). Cover and chill in the refrigerator. Marinate the wings for at least 1 hour or preferably overnight, turning them once.

Preheat oven to 450°. Arrange the wings in a single layer on an oiled rack set over a foil-lined roasting pan. Spoon the marinade over them, and bake the wings in the upper third of the oven for 30 to 35 minutes, or until they are cooked through.

BAKED MEXICAN RICE

Number of Servings: 4
Preparation Time: 30 minutes

Ingredients

1 onion, finely chopped
1 clove garlic, finely chopped
1/3 cup olive oil
1 cup rice
1 teaspoon salt
1 teaspoon freshly ground black pepper
1 tablespoon chili powder
1 (4 oz.) jar button mushrooms
8-12 slices garlic sausage or chorizo
stock (about 1 1/2 cups)
grated Parmesan cheese

Directions

Preheat oven to 350°. Sauté the onion and garlic in hot olive oil until just soft. Add the rice and seasonings and brown lightly. Add the mushrooms and sausage and enough boiling stock to come 1 inch above the rice. Cover with a tight lid and bake until the liquid is completely absorbed, about 35 minutes. Sprinkle with grated Parmesan cheese and serve.

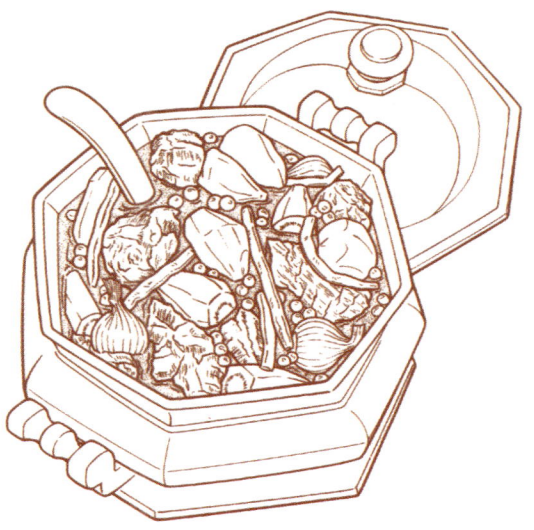

INTERNATIONAL

> "*A family* is much more than its individual members–it is the sum total of each individual's contribution."
>
> —Bishop T.D. Jakes

JOLLOF RICE

Number of Servings: 6-8
Preparation Time: 50-55 minutes

Ingredients

4 cups long grain rice
2 tomatoes and 1 bell pepper, or
8 oz canned tomato sauce and 3 oz canned tomato paste
1 onion, diced
1 teaspoon salt
1/2 teaspoon dry red pepper (cayenne)
1 cup chicken or beef broth
5 magi cubes

Directions

Put the rice and approximately 6 cups of water into a large pot over high heat. If using fresh ingredients, blend them until smooth in texture. Let rice cook for 10-15 minutes. Add either the tomato/pepper mixture or the tomato sauce and paste. Slice or dice the onion and add to pot. Add enough water to allow the rice to finish cooking (because the rice will not be drained, it is better to add too little and check on it often, than to add too much water).

Add broth, salt, magi cubes, and 1/2 teaspoon dry red pepper. Allow the rice to continue cooking until the rice is soft (but not too soft) and serve.

KAKRO

Contributed by

Number of Servings: 4-6
Preparation Time: 30 minutes

Ingredients

4 medium plantain, soft and very, very ripe
red pepper to taste
1/2 medium onion
1 whole ginger
1/2 cup flour
3 cups vegetable oil

DIRECTIONS

Peel each ripe plantain and slice into a blender. Blend until a smooth paste is formed. Pour into a deep pan. Wash and mince ginger, and add to plantain mixture. Add red pepper to taste and blend well.

Heat 3 cups of vegetable oil in a deep fryer. Using a small ice cream scoop or teaspoon, drop round spoonfuls of paste into the hot oil and fry until light brown. Remove and serve hot with boiled beans or cooked rice and stew.

FRESH FISH STEW

Contributed by

Number of Servings: 6-8
Preparation Time: 1 hour

Ingredients

2 pounds of fresh fish
12 ounces of fresh tomatoes
1/2 of fresh bell pepper
4 ounces onion, chopped
1 ounce of tatashe (red capsicum)
1 (8 oz.) can tomatoes
1/2 pint of vegetable oil
1/2 pint of water
1/2 pint of magi cubes
salt to taste

DIRECTIONS

Clean the fish, season, and steam for a few minutes. In a blender, mix fresh tomatoes, onion, tatashe, and pepper to a smooth paste.

Heat the oil in a large saucepan over medium heat. Add a little salt and then pour in the ground tomato mixture. Allow to boil for 20 minutes. Add water, magi cubes, and the canned tomatoes. Stir and add the fish. Cover, then cook for another 15 minutes. Add salt to taste, if needed, and serve hot.

INTERNATIONAL

MEXICAN CHOCOLATE TORTE

Number of Servings: 6-8
Preparation Time: 1 hour

Ingredients

1 cup natural whole almonds (with skins), toasted and cooled completely
1/3 cup firmly packed light brown sugar
1 tablespoon cinnamon
3/4 teaspoon salt
5 ounces fine-quality bittersweet chocolate, chopped
5 large eggs, separated
1 teaspoon vanilla
1/3 cup granulated sugar
4 ounces fine-quality bittersweet chocolate (not unsweetened), chopped
2 tablespoons unsalted butter
2 tablespoons heavy cream
1 tablespoon light corn syrup
1/3 cup confectioners sugar
1 to 1 1/2 teaspoons milk

Directions

Preheat oven to 325°. Butter an 8 1/2-inch springform pan and line it with a round of waxed paper. Butter the paper and dust the pan with flour, knocking out the excess, and set aside.

In a food processor blend together the almonds, brown sugar, cinnamon, and salt until the almonds are ground fine. Add the chocolate, and blend the mixture until the chocolate is ground fine. Add the egg yolks and the vanilla, blend the mixture until it is combined well (it will be very thick), and transfer it to a bowl.

In another bowl, using an electric mixture beat the egg whites with a pinch of salt until they hold soft peaks. Add in the granulated sugar gradually, and beat the meringue until it just holds stiff peaks. Whisk about one third of the meringue into the chocolate mixture to lighten it and fold in the remaining meringue gently but thoroughly. Pour the batter into the pan, smoothing the top, and bake the torte in the middle of the oven for 45 to 55 minutes, or until a tester comes out clean.

Let the torte cool in the pan on a rack for 5 minutes, run a thin knife around the edge, and remove the side of the pan. Invert the torte onto the rack, discarding the wax paper, and let it cool.

To make the glaze, combine the chocolate, butter, cream, and corn syrup in a metal bowl set over barely simmering water. Stir the mixture until it is smooth, remove from heat, and let the glaze cool until it is just lukewarm. Set the cooled torte on the rack over wax paper and pour the glaze over it, smoothing the glaze with a spatula and letting the excess drip down the side.

In a separate bowl, whisk together the confectioners sugar and 1 teaspoon of milk and add enough of the remaining milk, drop by drop, to form a thick icing. Transfer the icing to a small pastry bag fitted with a 1/8-inch plain tip and pipe it decoratively on the torte. Transfer the torte to a serving plate and let it stand for 2 hours, or until the glaze is set.

TOPICAL INDEX

BREADS

Banana Nut Bread - 120
Broccoli Cornbread - 118
Buttermilk Biscuits - 119
Mama's Sweet Potato Bread - 114
Meaty Cornbread - 121
Mom's Rolls - 116
Spicy Matzo Brei - 115
Zucchini Bread - 117

DESSERTS

Aunt Leanna's Pound Cake - 137
Banana Pudding - 135
Chocolate Delight - 138
Chocolate Iced Cake - 56
Chocolate-Hazelnut Waffles with Vanilla Ice Cream and Fudge Sauce - 141
Cream Cheese Flan - 126
Cream Cheese Pound Cake - 132
Don't Last Long Cake - 142
Dyan's Coconut Lemon Graham Cracker Bars - 48
Egg Pie - 136
Fantasy Fudge - 55
Flan de Queso (Cream Cheese Custard) - 139
German Chocolate Cake - 133
Glenn's Favorite Chocolate Sheet Cake - 125
Grandma's Favorite Pound Cake - 144
Heavenly Chocolate - 53
Heavenly Delight - 147
Jamaican Fruit Cake - 49
Les Brown's Vanilla Wafer Cake - 54
Lil' Rich Pound Cake - 140
Mexican Chocolate Torte - 156
Morning Glory Fruit Smoothie - 51
Multi-Chocolate Chip Cookies - 145
Neiman Marcus Cake - 124
Peach Cobbler - 57
Peanut Butter Thumbprints - 134
Pecan Pie Supreme - 131

Southern Pound Cake - 146
Sprite Pound Cake - 58
Stir-Fried Wild Berries - 50
Strawberry Dream Cake - 128, 129
Sweet Potato Pie - 52
Sweet Potato Pie - 143
T's Down-Home Apple Pie - 59

MEATS AND POULTRY

Adobe Chicken - 107
Angel Wings - 39
Baked Chicken Wings - 104
Chateau Briand Jubilee - 47
Cheesy Turkey Tetrazzini - 41
Crock Pot Stew - 106
Crown Roast Timothy - 99
Curried Goat - 108
Grilled Indian-Style Chicken Wings with Yogurt Sauce - 101
Grilled Lemon-Lime Chicken - 43
Jamaican "Jerk" Chicken Wings - 150
Joan's Barbeque Ribs - 105
Lucille's Chili Chicken - 44
Marinated Beef - 100
Roasted Rack of Lamb - 36
Russian Chicken - 33
Shepherd's Pie-Meat Loaf the Second Time Around - 46
South of the Border Rib Eye Steak - 38
Spicy Turkey and Rice - 109
St. Julien Creole Wing Fling. - 98
Stuffed Chicken - 110
Stuffed Herb Creamed Filet Mignon - 40

SALADS, VEGETABLES, AND SIDE DISHES

Baked Mexican Rice - 151
Broccoli Casserole - 12
Broiled Tuna and Raspberry Salad - 65
Cheese and Corn Pudding - 80
Chicken Soup Venezia - 21
Coconut Rice - 15
Crazy Beans - 82
Divine Salad - 10
Easy Fried Cabbage - 75
Favorite Seafood Quiche - 23
Glorious Greens, Glorious Greens - 73
Greek Salad - 11
Groundnut Soup - 16

TOPICAL INDEX

Irresistible Chinese Chicken Salad - 63
Joan's Greens without Meat - 72
Jollof Rice - 153
Kakro - 154
Lasagna - 25
Louisiana Cajun Style Dirty Rice - 83
Mexican Casserole - 13
Mexican Enchiladas - 42
Mory's Frittata - 79
New Orleans Red Beans and Rice - 81
Pasta Salad - 68
Queen Salad - 66
Quick and Easy Fruit Salad - 17
Sam's Chili Sauce - 69
Sam's Picante Sauce - 70
Screamin' Mean Greens - 18
Seafood Dip - 71
Selah Quiche - 78
Seven Seas Linguini - 24
Southern Chilli - 20
Spicy Artichoke, Baby Shrimp, and Orzo Salad - 67
Spinach Salad - 64
Stuffed Cannelloni with Spinach - 22
Sweet and Cheesy Macaroni and Cheese - 19
Vegetable Lasagna - 26
Vegetable Succotash - 74
Veggie Crab Salad - 62
Vickie's "Top Secret" Dressing - 14
Zucchini and Squash Medley - 76

SEAFOOD

Barbecue Shrimp - 86
Chilean Sea Bass with Shrimp - 31
Dawn's Dynamite Gumbo - 32
Exotic Southern Style Gumbo - 88, 89
Fish Gravy - 30
Fresh Fish Stew - 155
Honey Glazed BBQ Grilled Salmon - 37
Ja Nai's Red Snapper with Pineapple Salsa - 28, 29
Jambalaya - 92
Pan Broiled Fish - 95
Salmon Stir-Fry with Sautéed Vegetables - 35
Sea Bass with Curry and Ginger - 94
Seafood Casserole - 93
Shrimp Primavera - 91
Stuffed Shrimp - 34
Teresa's Fried Catfish - 45